RESCUED

&

RESTORED

KP

Edited by **Søren Roest Korsgaard** and **Caroline
Cheruiyot.**
Cover design by **Søren Roest Korsgaard.**

" One is absolutely sickened, not by the crimes that the wicked have committed, but by the punishments that the good have inflicted." -- Oscar Wilde.

TABLE OF CONTENTS

EXECUTING THE INNOCENT AND POOR – AMERICAN JUSTICE

Søren Roest Korsgaard

The death penalty is a humanitarian disaster. If you are to read a book written by a condemned man, we should, as a bare minimum, briefly discuss the implications of capital punishment. Setting other matters aside for the time being, the most important question, which needs to be addressed vis-à-vis capital punishment, is this: Is it infallible? Let us take a historical example.

At around 7 p.m. on June 16, 1944, 14-year-old George Stinney, a slim 5 feet 1 inch tall school boy, was manhandled by two police officers who were just doing their job and carrying out "the will of the people" of South Carolina. On this particular evening, they were forcing George down the cold and soulless corridors of the prison to a room with a single window. Behind the window sat several people on black plastic chairs, anxiously waiting for the officers to arrive with him. To the relief of the spectators, George finally arrived; some lit up a cigarette, others visibly smirked and attempted to get eye contact with the youngster. When George entered the room, he was looking straight at the hard contours of the electric chair, the preferred instrument of murder of the state at the time. Today, most US states that carry out capital punishment have settled on a toxic concoction of lethal chemicals that are administered to men and women fixated to a board, rather than the "old-fashioned" electric chair. The men of death discovered, much to their surprise, that poor George was too short for the electric chair. A few of their neurons fired and they rather quickly came up with a solution: The supposedly strictly religious men placed a King James Version of the Bible on the seat of the chair. Hereafter, they began strapping his four limbs onto the chair and then tightened a belt across his chest, keeping him firmly in place. Before leading George to the execution chamber, the men had inserted a wad of absorbent material into his rectum and attached a catheter to his penis. As the prison doctor and execution specialists prepared to murder him, they ran into other issues. The adult-sized mask, whose function was to protect the alleged sensibilities of the audience, was too large for his teenage face, and the prison doctor also struggled to attach an electrode to his right leg, which didn't need a shave beforehand.

All things come to an end, and as the massive jolt of voltage surged through his body it arched up rigidly against the restraints. The convulsions caused the facial mask to fall off, revealing that George was crying. The voltage was turned off, but he wasn't dead. The state executioner turned on the voltage again for a few moments. He was still alive. The heartless executioner turned on the voltage for the third and final time, killing him. The spectators were staring at the charred features of only 14-year-old George Stinney. His eyes were open but seemingly unseeing – saliva ran down from his mouth, and a small cloud of smoke, emanating from underneath the metal cap which had been attached to his head, quickly spread across the execution chamber and through the opening. By the time, the audience and execution specialists were breathing in particles of burned flesh, the prison doctor had pronounced George dead.

The prison doctor nodded at the observers, an indication that he was dead. Jubilation and celebration quickly spread across the room among the majority of the people attending the execution. Some praised the Lord while holding up a Bible in their hands.

In a matter of 83 days, George had been charged, convicted, and executed; the all-white jury had only deliberated for 10 minutes after a two-hour trial [1]. Seventy years later, his conviction was officially overturned as George was innocent. He had been brutalized into making a confession – an unrecorded and unsigned confession [2]. His incompetent defense attorney failed to "call exculpating witnesses or to pursue his right of appeal [3]." In fact at the time of the double murder, for which George was convicted, he had been in the presence of his family.

Today, almost 80 years after the execution, all is not lost as we can study the psychology of the participants and learn important lessons. As a bare minimum, the case is an example of police officials conspiring to frame an innocent child, even when the end result is *judicial murder*. In the Stinney case, the defense attorney worked on behalf of the prosecution regardless of legal requirements and morality. The most important conclusion is that innocent people are killed by the state – the "state" is a defuse term that in this case covers blood-thirsty and evil jurors, judges, doctors, and other prison officials who carried out the atrocious deed. It even went further than that as the governor, Olin Johnston, received countless letters and telegrams that pointed out the travesty of justice, and, accordingly, he should do his duty and pardon him. Johnston consciously refrained from doing the right thing and, thus, became a child murderer by implication.

In regard to psychology, it is more than interesting that people who murder with legal permission almost never show any guilt or remorse, which they, themselves, frequently demand from what they perceive as "actual criminals." For example, an assistant captain asked George if he had any last words to which he replied, "No sir [4]." A prison doctor couldn't believe it and urged, "You don't want to say anything about what you did [5]?" George replied, "No sir [6]." It is indicated that remorse and guilt are relative concepts.

It may be argued that absurd convictions and the like are things of the past. Racism and corruption were more prevalent in "the old days," etc. Furthermore, there is a world of difference between 1944 and 2020 – for example, condemned men and women are entitled to several appeals, meaning that they have time to point out errors made during the trial and present possible exculpatory evidence. It could also be pointed out that advanced forensic science is available today, unlike in 1944 when DNA and other scientific fields were science fiction. However, as we shall see, very little has changed since 1944. First, clear evidence that the US justice system is far from optimal has been presented by the eminent humanitarian organization *The Innocent Project*. This organization has assisted in exonerating numerous men serving life or death sentences in the US. These exonerated convicts were fortunate in that DNA was present in their cases. In many cases there is no forensic evidence, and we must also consider the possibility that police officials and technicians might plant and manufacture evidence against suspects they don't like. It is difficult to ascertain how many innocent people are on US death row. However, a study published in the *National Academy of Sciences* concluded that at least 1 in 25 on US death row is *innocent* of the crime for which they were convicted [7]. The scientists stressed that their study was conservative and the *de facto* number is likely higher. Similarly, it is difficult to estimate how many innocent people have been executed; however, the number is likely to be staggeringly high. Consider that in 1965 about 91% of all murders were solved, but today the number has declined to about 40% [8]. The reason the *homicide clearance rate* is much lower today is presumably that there is often not enough evidence to secure a conviction. Not long ago, people were frequently convicted without real evidence and then sentenced to death. However, as shown, wrongful executions still run rampant in the US as they do in virtually all other countries that carry out capital punishment, such as Saudi Arabia and

China. A recent example from the US might be Daniel Lewis Lee who was executed by lethal injection in July 2020. His final words were "I didn't do it. I've made a lot of mistakes in my life, but I'm not a murderer. You're killing an innocent man [9]." Lee always insisted that he had been in a different part of the country when the crime had occurred. The family of the victims strongly opposed the execution, but that did not make a difference. Long essays could be penned detailing numerous instances of judicial murder in the US and other countries. However, for the sake of brevity, only one more case will be discussed in some depth in the remainder of this foreword.

The State of Texas is a special place. First of all, Raul Cortez, who wrote this book, is on Texas death row, and, second, it is the state that is the most eager to execute people. Not surprisingly, given this statistic, it is also a fact that many prosecutors, state experts, prison personnel, judges, and jurors have their elbows soaked deep in the blood of innocent victims. For example, one of the most grotesque instances of judicial murder in Texas involves Larry Swearingen who was murdered by the state in 2017. Shortly before his execution, his appeals lawyer, James Rytting, stated: "They are going to execute someone that the legitimate forensic science has proven innocent [10]." Let's explore what Rytting meant. In the year of 2000, Larry was sentenced to death for the murder of Melissa Trotter who had been strangled with one leg of pantyhose. Joye Carter, the Harris County medical examiner, testified at the trial that the victim had been dead "25 days or so" prior to the discovery of her body [11]. The medical examiner later recanted her testimony, and in a 2007 affidavit she stated that the victim had died no more than two weeks before she had been found [12]. Several other experts, including forensic pathologists, forensic entomologists, and a forensic anthropologist, agreed with the two week time-frame

– which was determined by a variety of methods such as by examining insects found on the body [10]. This means that Larry Swearingen had been in prison at the time of the murder! He later said, "I was in no position, literally, to have committed this crime, as I was in the county jail [13]." As a nail in the coffin, in 2016 Dr. Victor Weedn, a forensic pathologist at George Washington University and former president of the American Academy of Forensic Sciences, released a detailed analysis that concluded that there was "considerable evidence to suggest that Ms. Trotter was not killed on the day of her disappearance, but was held, killed later, and her body dumped in the Sam Houston National Forest, sometime after the arrest and incarceration of Mr. Swearingen [11]."

How could he then be convicted, sentenced to death, and executed despite several appeals spread out over nearly two decades, you might ask? As we shall see, it probably happened due to a combination of incompetence, bad luck, evil, and especially that state experts and prosecutors were working toward bettering their own careers rather than justice. Let's briefly explore. During the trial, Texas crime lab technician Sandy Musialowski testified that another leg of pantyhose found in Swearingen's residence was "a unique physical match" to the one wrapped around the victim's neck "to the exclusion of all other pantyhose [11]." This would later be shown to be a deadly lie. Larry would later say that the pantyhose – despite being a mismatch – had been planted in his house by Officer Leo Mock. The prosecution called it "the smoking gun" of Larry's guilt [11]. However, the technician's own notes showed that she had found no match between them. After making this assessment, she began "working to make one piece fit the other [11]." Her incriminating notes were withheld from the defense team – the prosecution was in this instance determined to get a conviction regardless of Larry's innocence so they withheld the evidence – perhaps to bolster their conviction rate, or perhaps they didn't like Larry and wanted to get rid of him – i.e. murder him – and murdered he was at 6:47 p.m. on August 21, 2017.

Furthermore, a California State Polytechnic University professor of textile science concluded that the two hose "were cut in the same basic silhouette, [but] they were not cut from the same piece. These are not a match, and certainly not to 'the exclusion of all other pantyhose [10].'" Dr. Max Houck, a former head of the D.C. crime lab, later stated that Musialowski's testimony was "unwarranted given a deficit of scientific and statistical support for this type of comparison [11]." Obviously, Larry was innocent. But it gets worse. Much worse. The victim had scratched her attacker and underneath her fingernails were small blood flakes. A DNA analysis showed that it wasn't Larry's DNA. Unbelievably, during the trial, a crime lab serology expert, Cassie Carradine, dismissed the exculpatory evidence by inventing the notion that the DNA sample came from contamination [10]. Shortly before the execution, the Texas crime lab director, Brady W. Mills, released a letter in which he clarified that the assertion by the crime lab serology expert was unfounded [10]. In complete contradiction to the evidence, Montgomery County District Attorney Brett Ligon issued a statement that "anyone at this point in this process who believes that Mr. Swearingen is innocent is either delusional or is incapable of reading [14]." Despite manifest evidence of innocence, what can only be called, psychopathic Supreme Court justices decided to reject Larry's final appeal and murder him. If this is not evil, then evil does not exist. A short time later, Larry was poisoned to death while he complained of the chemicals burning his arm. In his final statement, as he lay with poisoned needles in his arm, he said:

Today the State of Texas murdered an innocent man. Many people participated in my demise, beginning with the Montgomery County police who falsely arrested me without a warrant and particularly Officer Leo Mock who planted the pantyhose in my home that was used to convict me. Harris County Medical Examiner Joye Carter then lied about the length of time Melissa Trotter's corpse [lay] in the woods. Judge Fred Edwards and the Montgomery County district attorney's office refused to give me a fair shake in legal proceedings, while the Houston Chronicle with other local media shared the same lack of fair play when it came to the court of public opinion. The Texas Criminal Court of Appeals rejected my filings without even looking at them, and finally governor Greg Abbott pulled the trigger […].

I have spent the last 19 years in solitary confinement, in a situation you wouldn't put a stray dog into. And this forced me to grow up. I found I had far more potential than I ever dreamed possible. I learned Texas law to the point where I proved my innocence beyond any shadow of doubt -- although unfortunately for me, actual innocence is not legal cause for stopping an execution […]. In closing, I want everyone to know I'm not angry about my execution. Sure I would've liked to live and go free. But I feel certain that my death can be a catalyst to change the insane legal system of Texas which could allow this to happen. I am now one of God's sacrificial lambs, and hopefully people will use my example to help keep others from experiencing this dreadful and wrongful persecution. With love in my heart and peace in my mind, I am yours truly, Larry Swearingen [15].

As with George Stinney, the victim's family cheered and celebrated while an innocent man was brutally murdered. Sandy Trotter, the slain teen's mother, proved to be particularly bloodthirsty and made no attempt to hide it from the media. Before the execution she said, "We are more than ready [for his execution] so hopefully it's looking more likely it's going to happen [16]." She also said, "We'll never have Melissa back and eventually his family won't have him [17]." She not only wanted to have Larry killed, but she appears to have wanted to torment his family. She also explained that she had plans to look him right into the eyes as he was being murdered: "I hope he's not too sedated," she said [17]. "I want him to know I'm there [17]." She even clarified that "He has had way too many appeals [18]." After the execution, she celebrated his murder – complete with a balloon release [17]. Likewise, Prosecutor Kelly Blackburn celebrated his demise and said, "A bad man got what he deserved tonight [19]." Where is the justice and morality in this? An innocent young woman is strangled to death, the perpetrator gets away with it, and then an innocent man is executed – while people cheer and laugh. It is no excuse to say that Sandy Trotter and others knew no better when they urged to get Larry executed and celebrated it afterwards. Due diligence extends to everyone. Unquestionably, numerous innocent people have been executed in the US – many of them after spending decades in solitary confinement, which is regarded as torture under the United Nations Standard Minimum Rules on the Treatment of Prisoners, i.e. international law which is above US law. Despite a mountain of evidence showing that Larry was innocent and tortured for almost two decades in solitary confinement, which is like being buried alive, no one has been charged with these offences – officially he is still guilty. If justice would be served today, the prosecutors, Supreme Court justices, scientists, police officers, the former governor Greg

Abbott, and especially those who facilitated and carried out the actual murder – prison guards, doctors, and the warden – would be charged with first degree murder, torture, as well as a litany of other serious charges. Lest we forget, how about the jury – should they go free for convicting an innocent man and ensuring his demise? The usual response to this question is that they were all "just doing their job." This rationale is moral blasphemy. During the Nuremberg tribunal, the defense offered by Nazi doctors, soldiers, and military leaders was more often than not that "I was just doing my job" or "I just followed orders." The rationale was so widely used that it became known as the "Nuremberg defense." However, people who commit atrocities for their government or any other person are not exempt from punishment, as explicitly declared by Nuremberg Principle IV: "The fact that a person acted pursuant to order of his Government or of a superior does not relieve him from responsibility under international law, provided a moral choice was in fact possible to him [20]." Obviously, Nuremberg Principle IV was violated repeatedly in the aforementioned case.

The two cases put forth in this foreword are separated by more than seventy years. There is a world of difference between 1944 and 2017 – yet the two cases are identical in many areas, showing that the US justice system has not changed much. However, advanced scientific disciplines have developed and matured in the past few decades, and convicts are no longer executed almost immediately after sentencing. So how can absurd judicial murders still take place? The answer is that morality and integrity of people in power stood still while the world around them progressed forward. In many instances, science has simply become a tool to advance nefarious agendas; Larry Swearingen's case clearly demonstrates how prosecutors hired criminal and/or incompetent scientists who supported their agenda, regardless of justice and morality.

And once you are convicted, it is almost impossible to get out, even with clear evidence – in the aforementioned case of George Stinney it took 70 years to officially exonerate him, but, of course, he had been dead for just as long. Those who are eventually cleared and released usually have to wait for two decades or more in deplorable conditions. If the truth about the abominable US justice system were ever widely disseminated, the public's trust in the system as well as in policy makers would decrease. Thus, there is a strong trend toward protecting the system at the expense of justice, humanity, and sound morality.

Science is often portrayed as a tool that is objective and without any authority, unlike a theocracy in which a deity is the supreme commander. This is a fallacy – often a deadly one. The reason is that those who are trained in applying scientific principles are no less prone to bias and corruption than you and me; thus, as we have seen, scientists often quarrel among themselves over the interpretation or significance of a finding. Evil prosecutors, like in Larry's case, may also hide or even destroy exculpatory evidence, compounding matters. The bias of scientists is best exemplified by considering that those who are working for the prosecution argue in favor of the prosecution's case, while scientists working for the defense team argue their case. Then there is also so-called "junk science," which is a term that covers pseudoscience presented as being robust and mature – or simply "scientific disciplines" that are falsely regarded as being accurate and reliable. Larry was killed partly due to "junk-science" and also "junk-scientists." He said: "If they kill me, I won't be the first man that's been [murdered]. I won't be the last. They killed Todd Willingham on junk science. I'm probably no different [21]." Cameron Todd Willingham was executed on February 17, 2004, for the arson deaths of his three children. Since then, it has been

proven that the fire was not arson, but just a regular fire [22]. Willingham was "convicted on the misinterpretation of evidence and Texas executed an innocent man [21]." Imagine having lost your three precious children and then be falsely convicted and sentenced to death? Could a more perverse instance of injustice even be conjured up by science fiction writers? No one has of course been convicted of murdering him – and psychopathic and bloodthirsty judges and jurors still vote for and impose the death penalty – 22 were executed in 2019 while 34 were sentenced to death. On January 1, 2020, a total of 2,620 people were on death row in the US. In many court cases, scientists do not agree. And at the end of the day, the frequently relatively uneducated jury is faced with two very different conclusions – and they have to determine which of the scientists they find the most reliable, or even likeable. Hence, life and death are often determined by whom they like the most, and so often that happens to be the scientists working for the prosecution. The reason is that the defendant not only has to fight the prosecution – but also the media, which has a long history of contributing to injustice, mostly in favor of the prosecution, but not always as seen with O.J. Simpson. Thus, frequently, jurors already have a bias or even believe that the person is guilty before the trial even begins. For example, in the case of Scott Peterson, the "written questionnaires of 1,000 potential jurors showed that almost half had already decided what the verdict should be, and of those, more than 98% of them believed Peterson was guilty [23]." Peterson's defense attorney filed a motion to move the trial to a different county. Unbelievably, the motion was denied. Pretrial media coverage included a "billboard in San Mateo County, showing Peterson in a jail suit, and asking people to vote on whether he was 'man' or a 'monster [23].'" So much for justice and a fair and impartial trial.
The law supposedly ensures a fair and impartial trial.

According to the Merriam-Webster online dictionary, the word, "impartial," means "not partial or biased: *treating or affecting all equally* [24]." However, how can this possibly be true when state prosecutors have seemingly boundless resources while average or poor defendants are frequently left with a limited and unskilled court-appointed attorney? On the other hand, the mega-rich can afford the best attorneys that money can buy. For example, O.J. Simpson´s fortune and fame ensured him the so-called "dream team," a team consisting of excellent attorneys. His money was well spent as he was acquitted notwithstanding detectives finding his blood at the crime scene and the victims' blood in his car and home. Simpson later gave a "fictionalized" confession to the double murder [25]. Prosecutor Vincent Bugliosi would later say, "In all my years, other than cases where the killer is apprehended during the perpetration of a homicide, I have never seen a more obvious case of guilt [26]." The quality of one's defense is a decisive factor, thus, studies have found that worldwide, not just in the US, poor people are primarily those found on death row [27-29]. According to the *Equal Justice Initiative*, more than 95% of death row inmates come from disadvantaged economic backgrounds [28]. Their underfunded and frequently incompetent court-appointed lawyers "often don't have the means to expedite the DNA or ballistics tests that could unravel the prosecution's case [29]." Dr. Philip Alston, who was appointed United Nations Special Rapporteur on extreme poverty and human rights in June 2014, has declared that the "death penalty has got a big sign on it reading 'reserved for the poor' [30]." Dr. Alston, who has also served as the UN Special Rapporteur on Extrajudicial, Summary or Arbitrary Executions, has also stated that "The death penalty is reserved for those who cannot buy themselves out of arrest, cannot afford legal representation, cannot afford a decent appeal, and carry no weight in the eyes of the government [30]."

Ndume Olatushani spent 28 years "chained and shackled like some imaginary monster [30]" in US prisons for a crime he did not commit. In twenty of those years, he was on death row. He later said, "All that time, I never met a rich person sitting on death row [30]." Ndume had been surrounded by family and friends celebrating his mother's birthday in Missouri on the night of the murder. He had never sat his foot in the State of Tennessee where the murder took place. Even so, the all-white jury found no evidence of his innocence and sentenced him to death. After his release, Ndume stated, "It is hard to imagine that any sensible person – with any humanity in them – will say that they support a punishment that is going to kill innocent people [30]."

One of the most formidable cases to illustrate the manifest impotence, corruption, and injustice of the US Justice System concerns the case of George Edward Mcfarland v. The State of Texas. His primary attorney, John Benn, slept through much of his trial. When the judge spotted the issue, he appointed a co-counsel, the incompetent Sanford Melamed who had zero experience with capital murder cases. Mcfarland was sentenced to death, although no physical evidence connected him to the murder – and serious questions have been raised about his guilt. During the trial, his attorney "only cursorily prepared for the case, barely consulted with co-counsel, put on no evidence and dozed through key parts of the whirlwind four-day trial [31]." Benn later admitted that the court proceedings were just "boring [31]." An appeal was later rejected by a Texas court, which ruled that "the Constitution guarantees the right to an attorney. It doesn't say the lawyer has to be awake [32]."

Why not take another example of the purported fairness and impartiality of the US Justice System? Mose Young, a poor black man, was convicted of a 1983 triple homicide. His court-appointed attorney, Jack Walsh, met Young just once four days prior to the start of the trial. Walsh complained that he had not had time to prepare. The judge had no problems with that. Walsh never visited the crime scene, and he conducted no investigation. Unbelievably, he even failed to interview a witness who said Mose was not the killer [32]. During the trial, Walsh "went drinking every night and came to court with a can of soda spiked with alcohol [32]." Mose always professed his innocence. On April 25, 2001, he was executed. Only the rich can afford an impartial and fair trial. A relatively more accurate mantra for the death penalty is that it is reserved for the poor, innocent, and unfortunate, rather than for the "worst of the worst." The national organization, *Equal Justice USA*, concludes:

> Poor defendants sentenced to die have been represented by lawyers who were drunk, asleep, or later disbarred. Others have been represented by collections or tax attorneys or lawyers fresh out of school. Some court-appointed lawyers can be so overworked or indifferent that they don't even bother to defend their clients at all [32].

Killing people based on an incompetent, ineffective, and sometimes corrupt judicial system is an outrage. The death penalty is irreversible – you can never go back once the deed has been done. Justice will always be imperfect; no matter what changes are made to the legal system, false convictions will never be eliminated – thus, abolishing the death penalty is essential for all intelligently governed nations. Even today, some governments enforce the death penalty on so-called witches, homosexuals, infidels, adulteresses, drug users, tax evaders, and on and on. It is essential that the US finally puts an end to the death penalty for humanitarian reasons as well as to send a clear signal to the international community that it is no longer acceptable. In short, judicial killing is wrong because (a) it is inhumane, morally corroding, and intrinsically encourages further state-imposed inhumanity and killing; (b) it is irreversible and, thus, denies the scientific approach to truth which is fundamentally about skepticism and critically testing potentially falsifiable hypotheses (indeed many innocent people have been executed because of this irreversible denial of the scientific approach); and (c) it excludes valuable humanitarian possibilities, such as (i) a redeemed and useful life for the prisoner whether guilty or innocent, (ii) psychological, genetic, and other scientific analyses of the convicted person for the benefit of all humanity, and (iii) other humanitarian possibilities for the convicted person (e.g. kidney or bone marrow donation if they have a rare tissue-matching compatibility that could save a life or lives).

As becomes clear from reading this book, death row inmates are held in isolation/solitary confinement. Although "isolation" and "solitary confinement" have been replaced by fanciful and deceptive terminology, such as "segregation," it is still, nevertheless, isolation. United Nations as well as human rights organizations have repeatedly scolded the US for its widespread use of isolation. In 2011, the UN Special Rapporteur on torture and other inhuman punishment, Dr. Juan E. Méndez, declared that "segregation, isolation, separation, cellular, lockdown, Supermax, the hole, Secure Housing Unit (SHU) … whatever the name, solitary confinement should be banned by States as a punishment or extortion technique [33]." Studies show that even a "few days of social isolation" can result in "lasting mental damage [33]." Furthermore, careful observation of the long-term effects of solitary confinement on US prisoners has revealed that it can induce a terrifying psychiatric disorder, which has been named, "SHU Syndrome [34]." This disorder is characterized by panic attacks, cognitive deficits, paranoid distortions, hypersensitivity to external stimuli, fears of suffocation, acute anxiety, insomnia, nightmares, perceptual distortions, illusions, hallucinations, intrusive obsessional thoughts, and "a litany of other physical and psychological problems [34-35]." Dr. Méndez's recommendations were later codified in the United Nations Standard Minimum Rules on the Treatment of Prisoners, known as the "Nelson Mandela Rules."

In 2014, Amnesty International published a meticulous report by the name: "Entombed: Isolation in the US Federal Prison System [36]." Pursuant to the report, the US "stands virtually alone in the world in incarcerating thousands of prisoners in long-term or indefinite solitary confinement [36]." It is estimated that more than 100,000 inmates are kept in isolation at any time. Across the US, super-maximum security facilities are designed to isolate prisoners indefinitely. While in other facilities, absurdities often lead to "segregation." There are examples of men and women being forced into isolation for using profanity, reporting rape by prison officials, possessing contraband, testing positive for drugs, ignoring orders, and reporting abuse by prison guards [37]. In 2010, it was reported that a group of Rastafarians had spent more than a decade in solitary confinement for "refusing haircuts [38]."

It is important to realize the urgency of the situation: As these words are being typed, innocent people are awaiting execution in deplorable conditions. We must all act now. Almost certainly, one of these innocent men is Rob Will. In 2012, a U.S. Federal District Judge concluded: "On top of considerable evidence supporting Will's innocence and the important errors in the trial court, there must also be addressed the absence of eyewitness testimony or strongly probative forensic evidence ... only circumstantial evidence supports Will's conviction and death sentence [39]." Rob Will remains on Texas death row.

Rescued and Restored is not just Raul Cortez's personal narrative. It exposes an invisible life to the readers as well as being a clarion call to society to examine America's criminal justice system. While the book is not about his guilt or innocence, Raul does mention that one of the jurors kept staring him down and would not take her eyes of him. In her questionnaire, she admitted to have "known the family of the victims for over 20 years." Raul reasons that if someone had "known my family for 20 years and had attempted to be on my jury, they wouldn't have made it past the questionnaire." Does that constitute a fair and impartial trial?

Søren Roest Korsgaard (b. 1986) is a social critic, humanitarian, and author. He serves as the editor-in-chief of CrimeAndPower.com and is the CEO of KorsgaardPublishing.com. He may be contacted via contact@korsgaardpublishing.com.

References

[1]. "It took 10 minutes to convict 14-year-old George Stinney Jr. It took 70 years after his execution to exonerate him." https://www.washingtonpost.com/news/morning-mix/wp/2014/12/18/the-rush-job-conviction-of-14-year-old-george-stinney-exonerated-70-years-after-execution
[2]. "The Youngest American Executed Wasn't Guilty" https://www.bustle.com/articles/54488-the-youngest-person-executed-in-america-george-stinney-jr-almost-certainly-wasnt-guilty
[3]. Ibid.
[4]. "George Stinney Jr. Was The Youngest American Ever Put To Death In The Electric Chair – Then His Conviction Was Overturned" https://allthatsinteresting.com/george-stinney-jr

[5]. Ibid.

[6]. Ibid.

[7]. Gross et al. "Rate of false conviction of criminal defendants who are sentenced to death." National Academy of Sciences (2014)

[8]. "America's Declining Homicide Clearance Rates 1965-2018," www.murderdata.org/p/reported-homicide-clearance-rate-1980.html

[9]. "U.S. carries out the 1st federal execution in nearly 2 decades after Supreme Court clears the way" https://www.cnbc.com/2020/07/14/us-supreme-court-allows-federal-executions-to-proceed.html

[10]. "Executed But Possibly Innocent" https://deathpenaltyinfo.org/policy-issues/innocence/executed-but-possibly-innocent

[11]. "Did faulty science, and bad testimony, bring Larry Swearingen to the brink of execution?" https://www.washingtonpost.com/crime-law/2019/08/17/did-faulty-science-bad-testimony-bring-larry-swearingen-brink-execution/

[12]. "Medical Examiners Lack Qualifications, Competence, Oversight" https://www.prisonlegalnews.org/news/2011/jan/15/medical-examiners-lack-qualifications-competence-oversight/

[13]. "Killer of Houston-area college student set to die Wednesday" https://www.myplainview.com/news/article/Killer-of-Houston-area-college-student-set-to-die-8732106.php

[14]. "'Lord forgive 'em': Larry Swearingen executed despite claims of innocence" https://www.houstonchronicle.com/news/houston-texas/houston/article/I-refuse-to-accept-this-as-my-fate-Larry-14366702.php

[15]. "POLUNSKY DEATH ROW- 'VOICE OF THE

VOICELESS'"
https://www.facebook.com/groups/719029064814278/permali
nk/2601213256595840/

[16]. "After 19 Years On Death Row, Could Time Be Up For
Larry Swearingen?" https://www.keranews.org/2019-08-
20/after-19-years-on-death-row-could-time-be-up-for-larry-
swearingen

[17]. "'I refuse to accept this as my fate': Larry Swearingen
slated for execution despite claims of innocence"
https://deathpenaltynews.blogspot.com/2019/08/i-refuse-to-
accept-this-as-my-fate.html

[18]. "After 19 Years On Death Row, Could Time Be Up For
Larry Swearingen?" https://www.tpr.org/news/2019-08-
20/after-19-years-on-death-row-could-time-be-up-for-larry-
swearingen

[19]. "Texas executes Larry Swearingen despite contested
forensic evidence"
https://theweek.com/speedreads/860444/texas-executes-larry-
swearingen-despite-contested-forensic-evidence

[20]. "Treaties, States Parties and Commentaries" https://ihl-
databases.icrc.org/ihl/WebART/390-550004

[21]. "After 19 Years On Death Row, Could Time Be Up For
Larry Swearingen?" https://www.tpr.org/news/2019-08-
20/after-19-years-on-death-row-could-time-be-up-for-larry-
swearingen

[22]. "Cameron Todd Willingham: Wrongfully Convicted and
Executed in Texas" https://innocenceproject.org/cameron-
todd-willingham-wrongfully-convicted-and-executed-in-
texas/

[23]. "NEWS: Scott Peterson Asks Court To Overturn Murder
Conviction And Death Sentence"
www.cliffgardner.com/_cg.php?news=yes&which=32

[24]. "Impartial" https://www.merriam-
webster.com/dictionary/impartial.

[25]. "O.J. Simpson Laughs While Confessing to Murdering Wife Nicole Brown & Ron Goldman"
https://www.youtube.com/watch?v=qJr24J3NmWo
[26]. "Vincent Bugliosi on OJ Simpson Pt .1 (1995)"
https://www.youtube.com/watch?v=eWhP7Jq2J-Y
[27]. "Poverty and the Death Penalty"
https://www.researchgate.net/publication/237669808_Poverty_and_the_Death_Penalty
[28]. "DEATH PENALTY AND POVERTY"
www.worldcoalition.org/media/resourcecenter/EN_WD2017_FactSheet
[29]. "The death penalty: a punishment for the poor?"
https://www.fidh.org/en/issues/death-penalty/the-death-penalty-a-punishment-for-the-poor
[30]. "Death row 'reserved for the poor'"
https://www.ohchr.org/en/newsevents/pages/deathpenaltyisabane.aspx
[31]. "Judge rejects appeal from Houston death row prisoner whose lawyer slept during trial"
https://www.chron.com/news/houston-texas/article/Judge-rejects-appeal-from-Houston-death-row-13751264.php
[32]. "Justice For a Few? A punishment for the poor"
https://ejusa.org/resource/poverty-and-poor-legal-defense
[33]. "UN Special Rapporteur on torture calls for the prohibition of solitary confinement"
https://newsarchive.ohchr.org/EN/NewsEvents/Pages/DisplayNews.aspx?NewsID=11506&LangID=E
[34]. What are the psychological effects of solitary confinement? https://solitarywatch.org/facts/faq/
[35]. "Psychiatric Effects of Solitary Confinement"
https://openscholarship.wustl.edu/cgi/viewcontent.cgi?article=1362&context=law_journal_law_policy
[36]. "Entombed: Isolation in the US Federal Prison System"
https://www.amnestyusa.org/files/amr510402014en.pdf

[37]. "Solitary Confinement"
https://mindfulnesspeaceproject.org/solitary/solitary-confinement/

[38]. "Rastafarians Spend a Decade in Solitary for Refusing Haircuts" https://solitarywatch.org/2010/02/11/rastafarians-spend-a-decade-in-solitary-for-refusing-haircuts/

[39]. "Free Rob Will" https://www.freerobwill.org

PREFACE

Dear Reader,

PEACE OF CHRIST

I'd like to take a few minutes, before you embark upon this journey with me, to say that my purpose with this book is to exalt the name of Jesus Christ in every way possible. I would also like to thank you, the reader, for choosing to travel through this journey with me. With that said, I would also like to quickly explain how this book came to be. I never intended to write my testimony in the form of a book. Originally, I wanted to write it for my family's eyes only. I wanted them to know how God had changed my life behind these death row prison walls. Yet as I wrote my testimony for my family, I felt the Holy Spirit put it in my heart to share it with the world. So I began *Rescued and Restored.* As I wrote my memoir, I purposely left out details of the case for which I currently find myself on Texas death row. Although, I do go into details about my state of mind before, during, and after my trial, I do apologize if my actions or words offend anyone who was involved in my trial and case. My main purpose is to exalt the name of Jesus Christ by testifying what He has done in my life. For this reason, I also omitted the names of all the occult books I studied along with details of the rituals I performed. I also left out many details of my gang activities. I did this not as a cop-out, but because I have no intention of promoting neither occult books nor any kind of gang activity. The only thing I want to advocate is the power in the name of Jesus Christ. Out of respect, I have also changed the names of everyone I have met throughout my journey. Lastly, I pray that you enjoy this journey you are about to embark on, but, even more, I pray that our wonderful Lord touches your heart at some point throughout this book. May our Lord and Savior

Jesus Christ continue to bless you all, today, and always.

Raul Cortez
July 20, 2018

DEDICATION

I dedicate this testimony to our Lord and Savior Jesus Christ, who shed His own precious blood upon the Cross at Calvary, so that we who believe in Him can share eternal life with Him.

I also dedicate this to my family who have been and continue to be by my side since my incarceration, always praying and interceding for me and lifting me up in prayer. May our Lord continue to bless them today and always.

I also dedicate this to the whole Body of Christ Church for having lifted my family and me in prayers. Your prayers have not fallen on deaf ears, thank you all, and may our Lord continue to bless you all today and always.

PEACE OF CHRIST

INTRODUCTION

I found myself handcuffed behind my back. My mind was still swirling from all the drugs and alcohol I had ingested just 20 minutes ago. How quickly my life had changed! For some reason, I continued to hear the words of a close friend of mine. I had never really given his words any thought. Tonight they sounded loud and clear as if he were sitting in the squad car with me saying, "Never let them put the handcuffs on you because once they do, that's it." Obviously it was too late for that, as I found myself in the back seat of an unmarked squad car. I was in the State of Florida, which was at least a thousand miles from home. Or was it really? I mean where was home? I had grown up on the Southside of Chicago, but had moved to Texas in the summer of 1998. Texas had never felt like home because I hated Texas. That was the reason I had jumped at the opportunity to relocate to Florida. Actually, I would have relocated anywhere had the opportunity presented itself as long as it was out of the State of Texas. I would be taking a ride back to Texas soon. It appeared that the State of Texas had issued an arrest warrant for me for a total of four counts of capital murder as I understood it in my dazed state of mind. That is a whole lot of charges, especially in a state like Texas that has a thing for executions. It was no wonder why my "takedown" had been so dramatic. Before I get too ahead of myself, I guess I should introduce myself. My name is Raul Cortez, and for the moment I find myself in a 6 by 10 feet prison cell at the Allan B. Polunsky Unit in Livingston Texas. I've been on Texas death row for almost a decade, but I have been locked up well over a decade counting the county jail time leading up to my trial. There are not many who can say that they have carried a death sentence over their heads for so long. These last 10 years of my life have been a real rollercoaster with too many highs and lows to count. I filled the first several years of my imprisonment with occultism, drugs, and alcohol while depression and death were always nearby. During those first several years, I experienced many things including coming face to face with Satan himself, as I signed my life away in blood pacts. I also experienced having an Angel of God standing before me. I have fallen to my knees in worship while cutting myself to produce blood for my blood pacts. I have seen many things that few can say they have witnessed with their own eyes. Death was always near me. I just didn't realize how near, until I found myself with a noose around my own neck, made and placed there by my own hands.

It is amazing the things we learn to hide from our families and friends by just painting a fake smile on our faces, and learning the right words to say. There is an old saying that goes, "Not everything that shines is gold." I know it is not a spectacular saying, but it holds great meaning to me. When brass is polished and shined it can be mistaken for gold, but when tested through fire, brass will quickly melt away while gold will only get refined through the blaze. There is also a verse in the Bible that I find similar to this saying. It is found in Matthew 23:27 where it says, "Woe to you Scribes and Pharisees, Hypocrites! You are like white washed tombs, which appear beautiful on the outside, but inside are full of dead men's bones, and every impurity." I lived a life like this for many years: Full of impurities and dead on the inside while moving about my life with a painted smile on my face. I use the word 'lived' because I no longer live this way. This was my life and this is my testimony.

CHAPTER 1:
DECEPTIVE APPEARANCES

Had someone seen me when I was in the free world before my arrest, they would have thought that I was the type of person who had his life in order. I'd worked my way up, in the company that employed me, from a forklift operator to a plant manager and then all the way up to a facility manager. I no longer got dirty at work and wore nice polo shirts with the company logo stitched on. I was invited to all the meetings with the owners, and my opinions carried weight. I'd come a long way from my first job at a soap packing company on Chicago's Northside. I wasn't doing too badly for a kid who had not even finished high school. My favorite part of the job was the traveling. I had the opportunity to travel from coast to coast. On several occasions, I even got the chance to travel on private jets or planes. On a few of those occasions, my bosses who owned the planes, and were pilots themselves, would allow me to pilot the planes. It was a major change from the life I'd lived growing up. I was earning more money than I'd ever earned before, and it was all legit. I had no wife and no kids. Kids were a big responsibility that I didn't really want to deal with at that time. I was having too much fun traveling the country and spending money. I only had one boss in the whole company and that was the vice president of productions. He was about my own age, and we had a good working relationship. I'd worked for him when the company still belonged to his family. They had recently sold the company to a corporation, and that was how I had gotten my promotion. My boss had promoted me when the company was sold. Some might say that I'd just gotten a lucky break, and perhaps I had, but I believe that I earned my position. I'd worked hard at my job from the very beginning. I'd been given responsibilities for shops in three different states and many employees.

Looking back from the outside in, it did seem that I was living the good life. I drove an elegant and expensive Cadillac with a nice sound system and a TV screen. I had a wonderful and loving family, and that in itself is a blessing, but for some reason unbeknownst to me, I was a broken man on the inside. While my life did look complete and good on the outside, and as if I was headed to some good places, it was all worth nothing where it really mattered. Some nights, I couldn't sleep at all. I would just toss and turn all night long. My body always felt tired or rather overloaded, even though I wasn't stressed. It was more of a mental fatigue than a physical one. I always found myself bored or anxious, always irritated, invariably looking for something to do, and I was never satisfied with what I had. Everything was getting so old to me. Everything seemed the same to me, though they might have been different faces and different places. The bar scenes, the strip clubs, the pool-halls, they just weren't doing it for me anymore. I knew there was something missing in my life. I just didn't know what it was. I was still young, just in my early twenties, but I'd been doing the whole bar scene since I was 16 years old. At 16, I'd gotten my hands on a fake ID, so by the time I turned 21, I'd already been through the club scenes and had moved on to the bar scenes. I had many of the things that this world tells us should make us happy, yet I wasn't happy, and I couldn't figure out why.

Since my childhood, I never really knew what peace was. Growing up on the Southside of Chicago, you learn things that you wouldn't learn in other parts of the country. You learn at a very young age to always be alert of your surroundings, and you quickly learn how to defend yourself. Growing up in certain neighborhoods in Chicago you never really have the chance to have a childhood. I'm sure Chicago doesn't stand alone in this. Feeling that I needed something or was missing something, I searched through many forms to fill the void. I wanted to take the boredom and emptiness away from my life and to tame my anxieties. I went through many bottles of alcohol and saw the bottom of many bags of drugs, seeking what I was missing. I'd go from woman to woman, but none of it made me happy. I enjoyed many material goods, drugs, alcohol, and women, but none of them could fill the void that I felt on the inside, and none of them ever lasted. Whatever I did, it would get blown with the wind when the morning sun would shine its lights. Then once again I would find myself having to start anew when the morning came, feeling even emptier than I had been feeling the previous night. Until now, the greater portion of my life had been spent this way.

I smoked my first marijuana joint when I was about 11 years old and had started drinking alcohol at about the same age. I didn't start off as an alcoholic and an addict. Instead, my tolerance began to grow with time, and it didn't take long before I began experimenting with harder drugs, and before I knew it, I'd become an addict. As an adult, not much had changed from my teen years: I continued to drink and use drugs. The only difference was that I had a steady income and had the money to support all of my habits and to give my heart and flesh all it desired. I did that in abundance. I understood and realized that my lifestyle wasn't doing me any good. It wasn't bringing me any kind of peace, and the joy from it had stopped a long time ago. Drugs and alcohol had just become the norm. They were a way to numb the inner battle that was being waged in me. For me, that was enough to justify my lifestyle and to continue down the same road day after day, though I didn't know how long I would be able to keep up at the same pace. The funny thing was that no one knew what I was going through. No one even had a clue as to the amount of alcohol and drugs I was consuming daily. I'd learned to wear a painted on smile on my face – always smiling always joyful, even though I was dying on the inside.

I cannot say that I never had any joy because I did have many moments of joy. I have many wonderful memories of times spent with my family that to this day bring a smile to my face. After those moments had come and gone, the next day, and in some cases the next hour, I was back on the battle field, which was my mind.

Coming from a Christian home and having two parents that are strong in faith and prayer, it only makes sense that I attempted to seek the Lord at different times. I would often go to church services and even play in the church band, but that was not what I wanted – I didn't want to be a "Christian." I wanted help. I just didn't want to leave my lifestyle in order to receive the help I felt I needed.

I do remember many times when I truly believe that I felt the hands of God. During altar calls, I believe I was liberated from the chains that held me bound, but as soon as I stepped a foot outside the church, I myself would pick up the chains and place them around my own neck. I wasn't disciplined enough, and I did not know how to hold on to my blessing. I had no real idea what it was to serve the Lord with all my heart, strength, and mind. None of this had ever really been explained to me. I didn't know that it is us who have to fight every day, and, at times, every single second, in order for us to maintain our blessing, our peace, and even our joy.

I had heard it said that our enemy is like a roaring lion looking for whom to devour, but those were just empty words to me that meant nothing. They were just words that I'd heard pastors say from the pulpit to get the congregation scared. I believed that once I gave my life over to Christ, it was He who would take care of the rest. All I had to do was confess with my lips that Jesus is Lord and that was it. Many years went by, along with many trials and tribulations before I understood and realized that Christ gives us the strength to go through any trial and tribulation, no matter how strong it may be. However, it is us who must put that strength to use. I have learned that there truly is power in the name of Jesus Christ. I only wish I had learned this many years ago. I've also learned that God is never late – He is always on time, and that all things work together for the good of those who love God and that even includes my death sentence.

CHAPTER 2:
THE ARREST

I think it is safe to say that everyone has what can be considered a defining moment in their life. Whether that moment comes in the form of a day, an event, or an action, will differ from person to person. I am no different in this regard. I also had a defining moment, and it came to pass on Friday, July 13, 2007. The day started like any other start to the weekend. I was living in Orlando, Florida, while temporarily managing a manufacturing plant until I was reassigned to my next location. That week, Orlando was hosting their annual "American Builders Convention." It was being held at the Convention Center in Orlando, and it is the biggest builders' convention in the country. The company I was working for had a booth that year, and I had been assigned to work it alongside the sales manager. It was easy work – just smile, say "hello," show people our products, and explain how easy it was to install them. I figured it would be fun, and maybe I could even get a few phone numbers. After all, I was single. After working at the convention that Friday, July 13, 2007, I met up with the sales manager, whom I had been working with, for a couple of drinks. While we were drinking, a stranger, pretending to be drunk, approached our table and attempted to engage us in conversation. He even went as far as ordering us a round of drinks. I later found out that it had been an undercover cop who had been tailing me. There was actually a whole squad of undercover officers who had been tailing me for some time. After we'd had a few drinks, we parted ways and I went over to another friend's house and picked up my drug supply for the weekend. Having what I needed, I went to my apartment and settled in for what I thought was going to be a weekend of drugs and kicking back. It was a quarter till midnight when I realized I had left my laptop at the office. I also noticed I was running out of cigarettes. I splashed some water on my face and headed out the door. I figured I could swing by the office, pick up my laptop, and get some cigarettes on my way back. I had the keys to the office as I was the plant manager. I walked out of my apartment, jumped into the company pickup truck, and was on my way. I maneuvered through the parking lot and headed toward the entrance of the apartments. When I turned a corner, I noticed a large number of law enforcement officers. They were standing in the middle of the parking lot forming a big huddle. The truck I was driving had a company logo down on both sides and across the hood, so it was easily recognizable. As I turned the corner inside the parking lot and headed toward the exit, I remember thinking to myself, "With that many officers standing there, someone is about to get raided." The neighborhood wasn't the safest around, so anything was possible. I just never imagined it was me they were there to arrest. As I passed the officers, I might as well have screamed at the top of my lungs, as they all turned at the exact same time and gave me a shocked look. Had I not been pumped up on drugs, I might have thought something was up, but the thought never crossed my mind that they were there to get me. I arrived at the entrance of the apartments and was going to make a left turn. I remember even coming to a complete stop and making sure that I used my turn signal, knowing that there were all those cops behind me. I made my left turn, and at about 50 yards ahead of me there was a red light. I was driving on the left side of the road. I was intending to make a quick U-turn at the light, and pull into a gas station that was going to be on my right. After seeing the cops, I really needed a cigarette.

I had also noticed that I was almost out of gas. I casually came to a stop at the red light, and within two or three seconds, there were flashing lights in my rearview mirror. From the time it took me to look from the front window to the rear view mirror and back again, I had become surrounded by law enforcement vehicles. I was now completely boxed in on all sides. There were many officers pointing guns in my direction. For a moment, the thought crossed my mind that I might unintentionally have driven into the filming of a movie, as I was almost directly in front of Universal Studios. But this was no movie! A tactical team had been formed made up of FBI, ATF, U.S. Marshals, Orlando Police Department, and Texas Task Force officers. They had been sent out to serve a warrant for my arrest. I kept my hands on the steering wheel and looked around me. I was surrounded. There were guns everywhere. They didn't really make me nervous as I'd had guns pointed at me in the past by both rival gang members and law enforcement, although I don't believe I had ever had that many guns pointed at me at one time. Most importantly, I was trapped! Even if I had wanted to ram my way out of there, the gas tank was nearly empty, and I knew I wouldn't get too far – that was, if I survived the wave of bullets that would be unleashed on me if I attempted an escape. I had to make a decision as to what I was going to do and make it quickly. I knew that they would not hesitate to blow me away, and it only took one officer with an itchy trigger finger and the rest would just follow. It was really just the drugs that were making me want to escape. I had no idea why I'd even been pulled over. Luckily, I came to my senses and slowly took my right hand off the steering wheel and put the truck in park. By that time, the tactical team had gotten a whole lot closer to the truck. I was blinded by all the lights that were being pointed in my direction. I looked out the driver's side window and an officer was standing about two feet away from me with his gun pointed at my head. With the truck in park, he told me to turn off the ignition, which I did. The drugs in my system were playing tricks on me. I told myself that this had to be some kind of mistake. All this drama just for me! I'd never even been to the county jail before, and I'd only had three speeding tickets since I was 18 years old. Yet from one second to the next I was being treated as if I was one of America's Most Wanted!

I was told by the officer closest to the driver's side window to open the door using the outside handle, and I did. I stepped out of the truck, and as soon as my foot touched the ground, there was another officer on me with his hands on my back and right shoulder pushing me toward the truck's side panel. I was quickly handcuffed, and then I was pat-down for weapons. Another officer came up to me and asked me what my name was. I responded by asking him what I was being arrested for, and he told me that I had a warrant out for my arrest out of the state of Texas for capital murder. I responded, "What! Capital murder! I haven't lived in Texas in over a year." He told me, "Well, you have a warrant out of Texas for four counts of capital murder." As he read me my Miranda rights, I was attempting to register what he had just told me. Had he really said four counts of capital murder? Another officer approached me, and asked me what my name was. I refused to answer. I had made up my mind quickly: From that moment on, I had nothing to say until I had talked to a lawyer. When I refused to tell the officer my name, a third officer approached us. This one had a piece of paper in his hands. He took a good look at me, and then told the others, "Yea, that's the guy, he's the one we're looking for." In his hands, he had a printed picture of me. I was quickly whisked away and placed in the back seat of an unmarked squad car. I could hear them talking outside the car about how easy a takedown it had been. I also saw them shaking each other's hands and patting themselves on the back, congratulating themselves. As I sat in the back seat of the car, I began to hear the words of an old friend of mine run through my head. I'd never actually given his words any real thought. It was now as if my friend was sitting in the back seat, next to me, screaming those words at me, "Never let them put the handcuffs on you because once they do, that's it." Obviously it was too late for all that. I was already sitting in the back seat of a squad car with four counts of capital murder hanging over my head – I still didn't believe I had heard correctly. Could it be that I was dreaming? I had been using a whole lot of drugs lately. Could I just be hallucinating? No, there was no way this could be some kind of hallucination because the handcuffs felt way too real. I could feel the metal biting into my skin. Could I somehow make a run for it, I considered. My goodness: Four counts of capital murder in Texas! I knew it was too late to attempt any kind of escape. The cuffs were on and they had me, as my friend would have said. Growing up in Chicago, I'd never even thought about the death penalty. Even though, during the 1990s, the State of Illinois did have the death penalty. However, I had never heard of it being applied. Well, I guess, it really made no difference now. I was cuffed behind my back and had been charged with capital murder. It looked like I was going back to Texas, and man I really hated Texas! After the dramatic arrest, I noticed that the onlookers began to scatter, and I saw my company truck parked in the gas station I'd intended to pull into. I figured I'd get in touch with someone from the company and let them know where the truck was parked. The way things were looking, I wasn't going to need it for a while or ever again. Once this hit the news media, which I had no doubt it would, I doubted I would still have a job, even if I was somehow quickly released. Two officers dressed in plain clothes jumped in the front of the car, and a third officer got into the back seat with me. The ride to the county jail was quiet and awkward. I couldn't even remember when the last time was that I had been in the back seat of a cop car. I was still high from the drugs I'd been ingesting just 20 minutes ago! Even with all the excitement, it had not brought me down from my high. In a weird kind of way, I was kind of excited as to what was coming next. I'd never been to jail before, at least not an adult jail. I'd spent some weekends in juvenile detention when I was a kid, but not an actual jail.

CHAPTER 3:
MADNESS IN THE COUNTY JAIL

I was processed into the Orange County jail by having my mug shot taken and having my fingers printed. My property was then inventoried along with my money. I was stripped searched and given a jail uniform. I'd never worn a jail uniform before, and let's just say that it wasn't very clean. I was also given a pair of worn-out shower slides, as shoes of any kind were prohibited. I did notice upon entering the jail that I was being given what I will call "special treatment." I didn't know it at the time that it was due to the severity of the charges. It is not every day that a man with four counts of capital murder walks into the jail. Being my first time in jail, I was expecting to go straight to a pod with other inmates. A pod, which is also known as "the block" by inmates, is a subdivision of a larger living space, e.g. the D-pod. Each pod consists of a number of cells, and is equipped with showers, cooking area, etc. However, before I was taken anywhere near a pod, I was escorted to the medical department to be evaluated. Although, I was beginning to calm down, I was nevertheless still high on drugs. My vital signs were taken and my heart rate was extremely high due to the drugs. After my vitals had been taken, I spoke to, what appeared to be, a psychologist for a few minutes. She asked me if I felt like hurting myself. I kind of laughed at her question. Why would I feel like hurting myself? I had never thought about hurting myself, so I responded in the negative. She then asked me if I felt like hurting someone else. I thought about that question, and, honestly, even with all that was going on and with all that had occurred, I really didn't have an inclination to hurt anyone, especially since my high was beginning to come down. What I really wanted was just to lie down somewhere and rest. She looked at my chart, which was being made, and noticed that my blood pressure was extremely elevated. She calmed me down, saying that it was due to all the action that had happened that night. She asked me a few more medical questions, like if I'd ever been committed to a psychiatric ward, if I'd ever attempted suicide, or if I was on any kind of psychiatric medication. Since I'd never experienced any of these things, I told her, "No." I signed several papers and was then on my way. I was escorted by two rather big guards with my hands still cuffed behind my back. I wasn't taken to a pod like I thought I would. I was, instead, taken to a room no bigger than a small walk-in closet. It was empty, except for a metal bunk and a stainless steel toilet-sink combo. There was also a thin mattress and a single sheet lying on the bunk. I thought a prison cell would be like in the movies with old-school prison bars. However, in reality it is just a small room. I went in and rested on the bunk. Sometime later, a guard came to the cell door and opened a small slot that was on the door. He then tossed in a sack lunch that contained two green baloney sandwiches and an apple. I had absolutely no appetite whatsoever. My high was fading, and my body was beginning to crave more drugs. I was exhausted as I lay on the bunk, but I knew I would not get any sleep that night. All I could do was lie there and stare at the ceiling, trying to make sense of what had just happened to me. Just a couple of hours ago, I had been relaxing in my apartment, yet now I found myself in a cage.

I don't know how many hours had passed by as I no longer had my wristwatch or any other way of figuring out the time. There were no windows to let me know if it was still night or if the morning sun had risen. It is a horrible feeling to even have the ability to tell time taken away from you.

At some point, I was escorted by two rather large and high ranking guards. I was taken to the unit's infirmary. This was a completely new experience for me. I'd never had a psychotic episode – neither had I ever met someone who had suffered from one. All of a sudden, here I was with about 20-25 men who were dealing with mental illness. I didn't ask any questions and went into the cell. My high had completely worn off by this time, and I just wanted to get some sleep. I figured I would deal with where I was after a few hours of sleep. I was awakened from my sleep by a nurse. I asked her why I'd ended up in the infirmary instead of a pod. She gave me a strange look and looked at my chart that was hanging next to the door. She then told me that I was on suicide watch. Suicide watch, I couldn't believe it! What were these people thinking? I wasn't suicidal! As if things weren't bad enough for me, they had just gotten a whole lot worse.

I didn't really understand the point of having me on suicide watch. Had I really wanted to kill myself I could have easily done it, but that was nowhere on my mind. I never again saw the nurse. The only time I would see daytime guards was when they would pass out sack lunches or trays. I only saw the night duty guards through reflection of the glass from the cell in front of me. They'd spend all night long sitting at a desk watching a small TV.

During my first night, I heard the cries of many ill-fated men pleading for help. At first, I didn't know what I was hearing. I went to the cell door, stood there for a while, and finally understood that the sounds were the groans of adult men. They were being tortured by their own personal demons as they were trapped, not only in those cold and lonely cells, but also in their own minds. My first night brought tears to my eyes. I was brought to tears because of the suffering I could hear in the voices of the tormented prisoners who were crying desperately. Some were crying out for their mothers, while others were just begging for help. I knew there was no help coming to their aid.

After a few days, the stress and frustrations of being trapped in a cell began to get to me. I had too much built-up energy that I was unable to release. In the free world, I was always on the go; I'd gone from being able to come and go as I pleased to being trapped in a cell. I hadn't spoken to my family for several days or to anyone else for that matter. I'd had no contact with the outside world whatsoever. I had not even seen the sun in days. I only knew when night time came because the guards would switch off the lights. At least, I thought it was night time – for all I knew they could have been switching off the lights in the middle of the day. Though I wasn't suicidal when I first arrived, if I had spent much more time in that cell there was a good chance I would become that. A few days later, I began to exercise as I needed to do something to burn off some energy. Being that I was on suicide watch, I had been stripped of my privileges, such as going to the shower. All I had to bathe with was a small piece of soap that I had received when I had first arrived. One day, I saw two inmates from the general population who were sitting in chairs, packing individual baggies with salt and pepper packs. I envied them because they were not being held as I was in a small cage. I desired so badly to just step out of the cage, even if it was only for a few minutes. However, nothing changed. I remained trapped in the lonely cell in the Orange County jail's infirmary.

There was always screaming in the infirmary at all hours of the day and night. It was like nothing I had ever experienced. One day the screaming got really bad. I walked to the cell door and looked in both directions, trying to discern the source of the noise. I was being held in a corner cell, so I could partially see the cells across from me and to my right. I was able to figure out that it was an inmate about five cells to my right, who had been making all the noise. I saw him as he was standing at the cell door, crying like a child, and pounding his head on the plexiglass door. I also noticed that he had written in huge childlike letters on the plexiglass, using smeared cheese from several of his sack lunches, "I LOVE YOU." I thought about his choice of words for some time. It was interesting that, instead of writing out curse words or drawing explicit images, he'd written the words he did. I wondered who he had written those words to, but even more importantly, I asked myself if he did have someone who loved him. I was dwelling on these thoughts when another inmate, who was in a cell directly across from me, got my attention. I hadn't even known that someone was in that cell. When I looked in his direction, he saw me looking at the inmate who was crying out. He made the motion with his hands to imply that the inmate was crazy. I thought about that too for a while. Was he just crazy? Or was he just lonely in that cage and perhaps in life?

He continued banging his head hard against the plexiglass door, screaming out for his mom. It was hard to take all of it in. Even though this was in the infirmary, and there were nurses coming and going, none stopped by his door to try and help him. They ignored him as if he wasn't even there, or as if he wasn't alive. Yet, there was no way that they could not hear his cries for help or the banging of his head. It made me think and ask, "Who were the truly heartless people in this jail, the inmates or the staff?" It wasn't until what felt like several hours later that a woman walked in and approached the cell. I can only imagine that the woman was some kind of a psychologist. She wasn't wearing a guard's uniform, but rather had on regular street clothes and a lab coat. She sat down in a small chair in front of the inmate's cell and attempted to calm him down. Eventually, she did succeed as the screaming and the head banging stopped. Perhaps she counseled him or, more likely, just medicated him in order to knock him out. When I left the infirmary several days later, the words, "I LOVE YOU," were still written on his door. It was a horrible experience to have spent time there. On the other hand, in a way it opened my eyes to a whole different side of humanity that I never knew existed. There were so many men in there with true mental disabilities, and keeping them housed this way was not going to help the prisoner or the society. If I were a gambler, I'd be willing to bet that their crimes had something to do with their mental disabilities. Sooner or later, most of the men were going to be released back into the streets, and I believe they would be worse off than when they had been arrested to begin with.

It was hard to keep track of the days I'd already spent in the suicide-watch cell. All my days seemed to just be running together as one never ending nightmare. One early morning, two guards unexpectedly showed up at the cell door. They told me I had a hearing scheduled for that day. I didn't have any kind of legal paperwork or anything else I needed to take with me, so I just splashed some water on my face and was ready to go. I didn't really care where I was going as I just wanted to get out of the cell even for just a few minutes. The guards handcuffed me in front and placed a belly chain around my waist, which was then secured with a master lock. Then they placed leg irons on my ankles and led me out of the infirmary. We walked down several long hallways and went up an elevator to an upper floor. When we stepped off the elevator, we walked a few more steps and I was directed into a small holding cell. And when I say small, I mean SMALL! The cell was probably somewhere around 5 by 6 feet and was empty except for a toilet-sink combo and a concrete slab used as a bench. I sat in there and didn't really know what to expect next. It had felt good to have gotten out of the suicide cell and just be able to walk somewhere, even with leg irons on my ankles.

I still hadn't had any real contact with the outside world or with anyone else in the jail for that matter, other than a few guards. I sat in the cell not really knowing what to expect next. I didn't even know what this hearing was all about. About 20 minutes went by when two guards showed up and told me they were ready for me. I thought to myself, "Who's ready for me?" I walked down the hall and went through a set of double doors into a courtroom. The judge was sitting on the bench in front of me. I quickly noticed all the TV cameras in the courtroom on my right side. I didn't know if they were there because of me, or if it was just the norm to have so many journalists in the courtroom. The guards who were escorting me pointed me toward a podium that was near the center. I had not yet spoken to a lawyer. I felt horrible standing there – I was unshaved, unshowered, and unaware of what this was all about, and to top it off I had TV cameras recording all of it. The judge then asked me some basic questions, and I answered them as best as I could at the moment. He then asked me if I wanted to fight extradition, and I told the judge that I didn't. I figured if my charges were in Texas, then I needed to get to Texas as soon as possible.

CHAPTER 4:
"YOUR LIFE WILL NEVER BE THE SAME AGAIN"

After that quick hearing, I was taken back to the jail, but thankfully not to the infirmary. The guards escorted me to a cell somewhere in the corner of the jail. It was about the same size as the cell as the previous one. As usual, the cell was empty, except for a metal bunk, a sink and toilet combo, a mattress, and two thin sheets. However, finally, I had certain necessities, like toothpaste, toothbrush, toilet paper, and soap. There were four cells in the corner of the jail, and I can only imagine that they were used as disciplinary cells. The other three cells were empty, and when I looked out through a small window in the door, all I could see was the empty cell in front of me. I couldn't hear any kind of noise or talk from anywhere. I had never been as isolated as this before. Did these people want me to lose my mind? The only time I saw anyone was when the guards would bring me food. There were a few times when the guards would "forget" to bring me my food trays; they probably just ate the food themselves or gave it to another inmate. The cell was beginning to really get to me. The combination of the isolation with the silence and the feeling of helplessness, were all starting to come down on me. I tried to sleep the days away, but my body could not lie on that hard bunk all day long. My back would begin to hurt along with the rest of my body. I believe this is when depression first began to appear in my life. A couple of days later, a guard came to the cell door and asked if I wanted to do a media interview. At first, I thought he was just playing with me or mocking me in some way as I still had no idea that my arrest had been covered by all the major news media in the country. I remembered the cameras in the courtroom, but I still hadn't put it all together. I had no desire of doing any kind of interview with anyone, and I told the guard so. He asked me to sign a waiver declining the interview. The guard returned several times in the following days as different media groups were interested in an interview with me. I finally asked one of the guards why all these media groups wanted to interview me. He told me, "Man you're a famous guy right now, your picture is on every newspaper and news programs in Florida." I was shocked to say the least. I still hadn't been allowed to get in touch with anyone in the outside world, as I'd not been allowed to purchase any commissary, so I could, at the very least, write to my family and let them know that I was okay. The "prison commissary" is a store from which inmates can purchase products such as hygiene items, snacks, writing materials, and so forth.

I had no idea what was going on in the free world. My family was constantly on my mind; had they already heard the news? I figured if the guard was telling me the truth, and my arrest was as high profile as he had said, then I was sure my family had already heard the news. I was worried as to how the news of my arrest had reached them, and how they had received it. I knew they were strong in their faith; however, something like this could push even the strongest of faiths to their limits. I tried to keep my family out of my mind, as I knew it would do me no good to worry about them. I couldn't reach them at the moment no matter what I did. So I tried to stay focused on what I could control. The problem was that I didn't know what was going on. No one would tell me anything, and I couldn't even talk to a lawyer since I had no way of contacting one. The four walls surrounding me were beginning to get smaller and smaller with every day that went by. I'd try pacing the cell from corner to corner trying to keep my mind active. I tried exercising but to no avail. It left me feeling famished and weak. All my basic rights had been taken from me in a matter of seconds, I hadn't even been charged formally with any crime, yet I was being treated worse than if I were in an actual prison. Was it even legal what they were doing – holding me this way?

I was pacing the cell one day when a couple of guards came to the cell door. I thought they just wanted me to sign another waiver for an interview, but they told me that a couple of detectives wanted to talk to me. I'd already determined that the only one I wanted to talk to was a defense attorney. I knew for sure that the last people I wanted to talk to were the cops.

I'd grown up on the Southside of Chicago where corrupt law enforcement is just an everyday part of life. I figured it was no different anywhere else. On the other hand, I really wanted to get out of the cell, even if it was just for a few minutes. So I went with the intention of not speaking to the detectives, other than to declare that I wanted a lawyer. Today, after many years behind bars, I can see the tactic that was used against me: They tried to break me by isolating me, putting me on suicide watch, and by not allowing me to get in touch with my family or anyone in the outside world. Isolation is a powerful weapon. However, it will only work if a person has a weak mind.

I went through the whole shackle routine again: handcuffs, belly chain, leg irons, etc. I was escorted down a couple of hallways, and then I was taken into a room with multiple filing cabinets and a small table in the center of the room with a couple of chairs. It wasn't even an interrogation room, but even this was all part of their tactic – they didn't want it to seem like an interrogation, though that was exactly what it was going to be.

Inside the room were two older detectives who looked to be in their late 60s or early 70s. I'd had a whole squad of officers who had been following me for a couple of months, yet they chose to send two old detectives to question me. I was directed to sit in one of the chairs and I did, but said nothing to them. The male detective configured a small camera on a tripod and pointed it at me. He turned on the camera and began to question me. Before he got too far, I politely told the detective that I had nothing to say. He looked at me and told me, "Mr. Cortez, you don't have to answer anything you don't want to, but you should really listen to what I have to say." He began to talk. For the first time, I was told about all the things I had been charged with. He obviously knew who I was – he'd done his homework on me, which wasn't surprising as they'd been following me all over Orlando for some time. He knew the names of my family members, which was just routine investigation work for them. Since he had done his homework on me, he was able to tell me many lies that had just a hint of truth to them. He told me lies, which I knew were lies, with a straight face, never once flinching or giving a tell. It kind of reminds me of the lying serpent in the Garden of Eden, telling a lie with just enough truth in it so it can be believed. Did God really say you cannot eat from any tree in the garden?

One of the detectives told me about how he already had others in custody and how "everyone" was pointing their fingers at me. He also mentioned my family in an attempt to sound caring and sincere about my wellbeing. I just sat there listening to the man give his best performance. After he did his best and saw that I still had nothing to say, he said something to me that made me laugh on the inside. It was something that sounded as if it was right out of the movies, but also something that demonstrates the corruption in our "justice" system. He told me, "You know how this thing works. The first one to talk gets the best deal. The others already have a jump start on you." For the first time in a couple of weeks, I had a genuine smile on my face. I thought to myself, "Who does this guy think he is?" Whether a person is innocent or guilty makes no difference, they are trained in the art of breaking people. In retrospect, I can see how they use persuasive words to play with people's minds. After spending over a decade behind prison walls, I have met men who have signed confessions to crimes they had absolutely nothing to do with. However, their tactics didn't work on me. The detective finished off by asking what I had to say to it, I said what I had previously told him: "I want a lawyer." One of them shut the camera off, I could see a look of disappointment in his eyes. I'm not sure what he had expected from me, but it was obvious he hadn't gotten it. He then turned and looked over at me with hatred in his eyes and said to me, "You think you're real smart, don't you?" I didn't respond. I had said all that I was going to say and he knew it. Then I guess he must have thought about it for a few seconds because he then said, "Well you are smarter than the people I usually deal with, but I will tell you this: Your life will never be the same again." And he was right about that because my life hasn't been the same since.

When they were done with their interrogation, I was taken back to the cell again. It had felt good to get out of the cell and stretch my legs even though it was a limited distance I had walked. However, I did have a heavy heart when I got back to the cell. I now knew what I was facing. The detective had mentioned the death penalty, and that was really the first time it had crossed my mind that I was actually going to have to face death penalty charges, but even worse was the realization that I had exposed my family to scrutiny. We have always been a close knit family, and even while I was away on business trips I kept in touch with them by phone calls every day. Although, I'd tried the best I could to keep my family suppressed in my thoughts, it became very difficult.

I spent several more days just wasting away the day. I couldn't sleep at night, so I'd pace the cell during the day in an attempt to burn off some energy. However, no matter how much pacing and working out I did, none of it was helping me, I was feeling empty inside. I was still holding on to sanity, but not very much.

I was staring at the ceiling one day as I did often. I still hadn't been allowed to even shower, let alone get in touch with my family. The only two times I'd been allowed out of the cell were to go to the court hearing and for the interrogation. As I lay on the bunk gazing at the ceiling, not really thinking about anything, I began to envision two letters in my mind. The letters were "RR," but I didn't know what they meant, but I was sure they didn't mean "Rest and Relaxation." I began to see these letters in my mind, day and night. I would wake up in the morning and the first thing that would pop into my mind was RR. It was also the last thing I would think about before falling asleep. I didn't know what the letters meant, yet I was becoming obsessed with these letters. This went on for a few days, until the meaning of them popped into my head. Out of nowhere, I began to see the words *Rescued and Restored* in my mind. I had no further understanding than that. The two letters had been replaced. Had I started to lose it?

For many years, I have been asking myself about the meaning of the words. Perhaps they signify the name of a ministry that God has planned for me or if it was the plans He had for my life – because at the end of the day that was exactly what He did for me: He rescued and restored me completely.

My mind was under constant stress and I felt that it was playing tricks on me. It was presumably the combination of isolation and the lack of drugs and alcohol in my system, not to mention the charges I was facing and the constant thoughts of my family. No matter how much I tried to suppress the thoughts and constant worries I couldn't do it. In a moment of loneliness and despair, I cried out to God in a plea for help, but it wasn't really a sincere plea for help – I realize that today. It was only the situation I found myself in and the frustrations of being in that cell that had made me do it. God is not a genie in a bottle whom we can call on only in our times of need, while living the rest of the time as if there is no God.

Several days later, I was finally allowed to shower. The simple act of taking a shower renewed me like no shower had ever done before. I stayed in that cell for the remainder of my time in the Orange County jail. A couple of guards appeared at the cell door one early morning. They told me that *Texas* had arrived to get me. I went through the shackle routine and was escorted to a transfer cell on the first level of the jail. I waited there for several hours until the bright morning sun came up. From this cell, I could finally see the sunlight. I hadn't seen it in a couple of weeks and didn't really know how much I had missed it, until I saw it again. It somehow made me feel better inside. I suddenly felt as if everything was going to be okay. There were two Collin County sheriffs to pick me up. When the sheriffs arrived, I was handed over to their custody. I was again reshackled and placed in the back seat of an unmarked car. I was now on my way back to Texas to face capital murder charges and possibly the death penalty. I'd have to take it one step at a time. On the bright side, I would be closer to my family and would probably find a way to see them.

It is somewhere around a 16 hour-drive from Orlando, Florida, to McKinney, Texas, where the Collin County Jail is located. This was the longest drive of my life. Being shackled for that amount of time should be considered a cruel and unusual punishment if you ask me. We did make a few stops, every time the car needed refueling. At one point, when we entered the State of Texas, we stopped at a fast food restaurant for a quick bite. I was asked if I needed to use the restroom and I told the sheriff that I did, though all I really wanted was to stretch my legs out. I was escorted into the restaurant and I ordered fries, a burger, and a bottle of water. It just so happened that the restaurant had a small TV on a stand near the dining area. When I walked in, I was shackled up and looked disheveled from weeks of not shaving. At that very moment, the TV was turned on to the local news channel. As luck would have it: On the screen was my picture while they were talking about my case. The young man at the counter looked at me – he then slowly turned and saw the picture on the screen and quickly put one and one together. His mouth dropped in a state of disbelief. The sheriffs immediately sensed what had occurred and before I could finish my food, they ushered me to the restroom and back to the car as quickly as possible. That was the last meal I had outside of prison. We were on our way again.

CHAPTER 5:
THE BIG SHOW BEGINS

I arrived at the Collin County jail in McKinney, Texas, sometime in the middle of the night. I had to once again go through the whole intake process – I had new mug shots taken and was fingerprinted. The new mug shot was obviously the one that was used to identify me by the news media. I hadn't shaved in weeks and had just gotten off a 16-hour-drive. It's as if they wanted to paint the worse possible picture of me. So much for innocent until proven guilty. After I was processed into the system, I was taken down several long hallways and up an elevator. I was still fully shackled making it hard for me to take long steps. So it took us a while to get to where we were going. When we finally arrived at a pod, all the lights were turned on at our arrival. Some of the inmates woke up and came to the cell doors to see what was going on. I was instantly surprised that there were people who knew who I was. As I walked toward the cell I'd been assigned, there was a young Hispanic male standing at his cell door. He said, "What's up Cortez?" I didn't respond to him as I was sure I didn't know who he was. I was wondering how he knew who I was. I walked into the cell and was immediately relieved. The cell was much bigger than the cells I'd been housed at in Orlando. I also quickly noticed that there was a shower inside the cell, and I saw a phone on the wall and a TV mounted on a brace attached to the wall. I was really excited at seeing the phone as I wanted to get in touch with my family, at the very least just to let them know that I was okay.

The guards removed the shackles from me and left me to myself. I walked to the cell door, which consisted of a metal frame, but had the upper and lower halves made of plexiglass. It also had a slot built into the center of the door. The cell already had a mattress and sheets inside when I had walked in.

I had been given a small plastic bag that had a toothbrush, toothpaste, and a small bar of soap.

I saw the guy, who had greeted me, still standing at the door, and I asked him how he knew my name. He just smiled and told me that everyone in McKinney knew my name. I took that in for a few seconds, still not really sure what he meant by that. He told me his name was Julio. I asked him what he meant by everyone in McKinney knew my name. He told me that for the last couple of weeks they had been putting my picture on every news channel and newspaper in Texas. It was all hard for me to take in. I was hearing his words, but they just weren't really registering in my head. I didn´t want any publicity or media attention. I walked away and went to bed. It had been a tough couple of weeks and a long drive from Orlando to McKinney. I was awoken several hours later at breakfast time. When the guard handed me a breakfast tray, he also handed me a few hygiene items that Julio had sent me. I ate my breakfast and jumped straight into the shower. It felt good to have that basic privilege again. When I got out of the shower, I turned on the TV. I was curious to see what Julio had been talking about. It became obvious almost immediately. The very first thing I saw was my new mug shot, just a few hours old. Word had gotten out that I had arrived in Texas. At that moment, I finally understood exactly how high profile my arrest had actually been. A few hours later on that first day, a guard came on the intercom that was in the cell. He told me I had a visitor. I wondered who that person could be because I had just arrived a few hours ago. It crossed my mind that perhaps it was a TV station wanting an interview, which I was not prepared to give. Then I thought about my family. Could it be someone from my family? I had put them on my visitation list that morning when I'd been processed in. As I was mulling over who it could possibly be, two guards arrived with all the usual chains and shackles. I was escorted to the visitation area, and I noticed that I was receiving the same "special treatment" as I had received in the county jail in Orlando. I later found out that the special treatment is called, "keep away from all," and it is a classification status for high risk prisoners. This was my first time in jail and I was already classified as a high risk. It didn't really make any sense to me, but what could I do? I walked to the visitation area which was about 30 feet from the pod I was in. As soon as I walked in, I saw my sister on the other side of a plexiglass wall. My heart skipped several beats at just seeing her standing there. I was so happy to see her that words could not describe what I was feeling at that moment. All I wanted to do was run to her and throw my arms around her in a warm embrace. She saw me walk in, and even though she saw all the chains and shackles on me, she gave me the biggest and warmest smile I have ever received. Just seeing that smile lifted my spirits in ways that I can't begin to explain. It is amazing the effects a person can have on another human being by just letting themselves be seen. I can't begin to imagine what must have gone through her mind as she saw me chained up, worse than an animal. Yet through it all, she held her own pain and feelings inside. We were allowed a 20 minute visit. We were seeing each other through a plexiglass and using phones on both ends to communicate. I asked her how the family was doing. She told me that they were all dealing with it in the best way that they could, which was understandable. She told me that my brother had been arrested, but this I already knew as the detective in Orlando had told me that during my interrogation.

Though my spirits had been lifted for the first time in a couple of weeks, it was hard for me to say goodbye and see her walk out of the visitation area. I was escorted back to the cell and went to bed. I thought about my mother and father and what they must have been going through. I thought about my brother and how he was holding up. I thought about all my nieces and my nephew. I had not given myself time to dwell on any of this while I was in Orlando, but the time had come. When Julio had his recreation or exercise time, he came to the cell door and we talked for a while. He gave me a breakdown of how the county jail worked: the visitation times, the phone usage, and how the whole trial was supposed to go. It sounded like Julio wasn't new to the court system. I realized that there was not much I could do until I had a lawyer appointed.

That same day I got a second visit, this time it was an attorney's visit. It wasn't my lawyer, but it was actually my brother's attorney. He'd come to give me an important advice, though it was not a revelation of any kind. He was simple but direct, he said, "Keep your mouth shut – don't talk about your case to anyone." He also advised me to stay away from media interviews and other prisoners as the state is always looking for jailhouse snitches. Lastly, he suggested that I should just sit tight until I had a lawyer appointed. I asked him about my brother, and he told me that my brother was doing just fine. He told me not to worry about him and to try not to stress myself out too much. I then went back to my cell.

My mind was just beginning to clear up from all the years I'd spent ingesting drugs and alcohol. These had been the first several weeks in a row that I'd gone without doing drugs or drinking alcohol in many years.

It took several weeks before I was finally appointed a lawyer. He came to visit me, but he told me that he was unable to remain my lawyer due to some kind of conflict of interest. He then basically told me the same thing as my brother's attorney. A couple of weeks later, I was finally appointed a lawyer who had no conflict of interest and would represent me during my trial. Seeing how this was a pretty big case, he had brought along two additional lawyers to assist with the case. I met with all three of them and they sounded as if they had my best interest at heart. Whether they did or not is debatable, but that is a story for another time. This was the first time I'd ever been in any kind of real trouble. I'd gotten into some minor mischief as a juvenile, but never as an adult. I didn't really know how the "system" worked. The only experience I had with the legal system came from watching courtroom dramas on TV. Based on what I had seen on TV, I reasoned that lawyers really want to fight for their clients, but it was nothing like that in real life. In reality, the cards are stacked against you from the very start: The prosecution has an unlimited amount of funds and man power. Furthermore, while the judge is supposed to be unbiased, he or she will usually favor the prosecution's side. After all, judges are elected and thus don't want to be seen as being soft toward alleged criminals. One thing, that my lawyers did tell me, was that it would be a slow process and to a certain degree it was. However, even this was just a part of a big show, such that it looked good in the eyes of the public. I sat in the county jail for a total of 19 months. During my time, I pretty much kept to myself, not talking about my case. I've always been somewhat asocial; thus, not interacting with the people around me wasn't a big deal. Growing up, I always had a small circle of friends as I was never really into the big crowd scene. In prison, I was a "keep away from all," which meant I was allowed to exercise for one hour per day, but alone. Every time I left the cell for anything, I had to be incapacitated by chains and handcuffs, making it extremely difficult for me to exercise or do anything being chained, like an animal, so I didn't go to the exercise area frequently. Eventually, I was allowed to go there without all the irons being placed on me. It was then that I really got to know the men who were around me, though I made absolutely certain that I never mentioned anything about my case. Although, I was new to jail life, I wasn't new to the game. Prison is full of all kinds of different attitudes and characters. There are men of different body sizes and ages, and the county jail is no exception to this. Everyone does their own time differently from each other. For the most part, the older inmates do their time easier. They are more laid back while younger inmates come to jail with lots of energy and peeking levels of testosterone, and do their time more actively, so to speak. To me, it really made no difference as I was still physically isolated from the others.

I became good friends with some of the men who were there for the long haul as I was. We were housed in what is called the "SHU" (Special Housing Unit). Some were there because they had caused too many fights out in the general population, while others because they were scared to be among the other prisoners, usually due to allegations of child molestation. Others were housed in the SHU because they were snitching on co-defendants or other inmates. I and a few others were there because we had high profile cases. Inmates were constantly coming and going, as some would sign plea deals and catch a chain bus to prison. Others would take it to trial and get sentenced, while others would just get bail or get released. It was a constant flow of men coming and going through the system.

One of my neighbors was Polo, he, too, was facing multiple capital murder charges. Though in his case the state was not seeking the death penalty by execution, rather he was facing a different kind of death sentence: Life without the possibility of parole. Personally, I don't know which one is worse: death by execution or death by other causes in prison. Polo was a couple of years younger than I was, and he was from Vera Cruz, Mexico. Due to his charges, he was also going to be there for a while as he was taking it to trial. We remained neighbors for some time as both of our cases slowly made their way through the system. Polo wasn't a proficient English speaker, so it was hard for him to communicate with his attorneys. I tried to help him as much as I could with his legal letters, despite being new to the system. Polo and I spent the next several months standing at the cell doors talking to each other when we were not out of the cell. The way the cells and pod were designed, we could hear each other talk, but we could not see each other as the cells were right next to each other. We could also have used the vent system to talk through, but those conversations would have been heard by everyone else nearby. Polo and I became good friends. We were both in similar situations and were both about the same age. He'd tell me all about his family and about growing up in Mexico, and I would likewise share stories with him about growing up on the Southside of Chicago. They sounded like two different worlds. Polo once mentioned to me that his grandparents still lived in Vera Cruz. He told me that they lived in a small town known for witches and the practice of black magic. His grandparents were also practitioners of black magic. Looking back at our conversations, I never thought anything of them. To me, they were just conversations between two friends who were facing similar situations at that moment. All we were doing was killing time by sharing our life stories with each other and getting to know each other. Years later, I came to understand and realize that those simple conversations were not as innocent as they seemed. I've since then come to believe that they were in all actuality seeds that Satan was planting in my mind and heart. If the Word of God is correct, which I believe it is, and faith comes by hearing the word of God (Romans 10:17, NIV), is it not also possible that evil may come through the hearing of evil? I believe that Satan was planting these seeds of evil in me, hoping that down the line they would give fruit, and fruit they did give. Slowly, but surely, without my knowledge, depression began to develop in my mind and soul. I had no idea what depression even was. I'd heard it mentioned from time to time from people around me. However, I had no idea what the symptoms of depression were or how depression was even developed. My mom and dad were strong in their faith, and they continued to march forward in the spiritual and physical battles, they, too, were facing. They came to visit me every week, always encouraging me with the word of God. At times, they would spoon feed me the word of God, and, at times, even force me to listen to it. I am truly grateful to have been blessed with loving parents who are strong in faith and love of the Lord, even if, at the time, I didn't realize what a blessing they were. There were times when I would return to the cell and their words would hit a soft spot in my heart, and I would seek the Lord's face and His word, though it was never a sincere plea. It was never really a true plea of repentance as it was always driven by the situation I found myself in. Besides, I believe God already had His own plans for my life, and His purposes were not going to be interrupted.

As the days turned into weeks and the weeks into months, I continued having conversations with Polo and others that would come and go. There were some who I actually saw get released, only to come back months later. As time went by, I was falling deeper and deeper into depression, but something else was also beginning to grow within me. I've never been the type of person to hold a grudge for too long. Yes, there have been many times I've gotten really upset with someone, but it has never lasted, even in the streets of Chicago where I sometimes got beat up by rival gang members. I understood that it was just a part of growing up in the hood. Whether it was a combination of the isolation mixed with the depression, along with the charges I was facing, I am not sure, but seeds of anger and hatred had begun to grow in me like never before. One step at a time, Satan was planting his seeds deeply inside my heart.

CHAPTER 6:
SATAN IS AN INTELLIGENT BEING

May our God continue to bless my family for all their love, courage, and strength. They continued to visit me every time they were allowed to do so. I'd always attempt to hide my emotions from them along with everything that was going through my mind. In retrospect, I realize that my family was fighting their own battles at the same time that I was stuck in my cell. Even today, they continue to fight battles as they carry my death sentence along with me. There were many times that I was at my worst, but because of their love and prayers to our God, He held me up through those times, but as I wasted away inside my cell, the seeds that Satan had planted were beginning to take root. One otherwise seemingly normal evening became very significant. In retrospect, I can see that depression had begun to take a toll on me. I didn't know something was seriously wrong with me, as I just assumed it was normal for me to be feeling this way, and to feel the palpable anger that I was experiencing. After all, I was facing four counts of capital murder, I'd lost a great job, and I was being held in isolation. It didn't help that I continued to hear my attorneys say "death penalty" every time I spoke to them. I didn't know, nor do I know now, what it was that propelled me into making a decision that would affect me for the rest of my life. I was depressed and so full of rage that I got off the bunk, dropped to my knees, and began to worship Satan. I didn't know how this was supposed to help me or if it was supposed to help me in any way. I acted on an impulse and that sent me to my knees, and words of worship began to flow from my lips.

Satan is an intelligent being. The Bible states in Ezekiel 28:12 (NIV) that "[Satan is] full of wisdom and perfect in beauty." I have learned firsthand that he is patient to get what he wants.

He also knows all of our weaknesses and when we find ourselves at our weakest moments. He has been studying the human race for millenniums and has brought down many a great man. Satan easily penetrated my mind and heart, as I had put up no defenses. At that time, I had never practiced occultism. In fact, I'd been raised in a Christian home with parents that were staunch Pentecostals. I had been instilled with the belief of an actual spiritual world, even if I didn't understand how it worked or how it could affect the natural world. Yet from that day onward, I began to worship and pray to Satan every day. Perhaps it was all in my mind, but when I began to worship Satan, I began to see a difference in what my attorneys began to tell me. It was as if their attitudes toward my case had changed. They actually began to talk about having me back home before the end of the year.

At the Collin County jail, it was prohibited for us to have a shaving razor. We were not even allowed to have magazines that had staples on them. While I was looking through my legal paperwork one day, I found a staple that the guards had missed when they had brought me the documents. I picked it up, and the next thing I knew was that I was on my knees sharpening the staple on the concrete floor. I acted on an impulse rather than careful thought. After I had sharpened it to the best of my ability, I began to poke it at my left index finger until I had made a nice cut at the tip. Using a wrapper from a soup pack, I collected the blood that was dripping from the tip of my finger. Then, using an empty pen, I began to dip the tip of the pen in the blood and write out a blood pact with Satan on a piece of paper. I wrote the whole thing using my own blood and signed it with it as well. I had to poke several more times as I ran out of blood while I was writing. That was my first of many pacts I would make and sign not only with Satan, but with many of his fallen angels.

My family continued to faithfully visit me every week. I

remember that my attitude towards my family had become extremely negative and even demonic as I hated to hear the name of Jesus Christ. Every time my mom and dad would visit, they would greet me with, "God bless you." For some reason, it would burn me up inside to hear those words. Yet I had to endure them at the beginning and end of each of our visits. At the end of our visits, they would stand there and stare at me, waiting for me to give them the same blessing. I couldn't do it. I couldn't get the words out of my mouth. At one point, I told my mother that I was not going to bless anyone. I could see the pain and hurt in her eyes every time I said things like that. After some time, I began to have some really strange dreams, which I believe were caused by a mixture of both my depression and the demonic influence I was inviting into my life.

I was eventually moved to another section of the jail for reasons that I do not know. It was still in a "SHU-pod," although the cells were somewhat different. On this pod, the cell doors were fully covered, apart from a small window on the upper half. I remember lying on the bunk one day, watching TV, when something at the window caught my eye. I looked toward the small window on the cell door, and standing there was a demon observing me. It had a blank expression in its eyes as it looked straight into mine. I was too stunned to move or scream or do anything. I just lay there on the bunk looking at the demons and its terrifying eyes, and just like that it walked away without saying a word to me. I was completely awake when this occurred and couldn't believe what I had just seen. This was only the beginning. My depression continued to grow more and more every day. I found that there were days I had no energy to even get off the bunk. Or maybe it wasn't that I lacked energy, but rather lacked desire to get up. What I managed was to lie on the bunk, watch TV, and eat. My attorneys would visit me from time to time, and they continued to tell me about all the things they were finding in my favor. Unfortunately, none of those "good" things were ever introduced at my trial. The more they continued to tell me, the more I continued to bend my knees in worship toward Satan. At night, I could feel a demonic presence in my cell.

During the jury selection or voir dire, as it also is called, the people who had been called in expressed nothing but hatred toward me – people I'd never met. The media had painted me in a way that there was no way I could ever receive a fair trial. Words like "death sentence" and "lethal injection" continued to be thrown around as if discussing a theme park ride. It went on this way throughout the entirety of the jury selection. I could hear their judgmental responses to our questions in their voices, and I could see the hatred in their eyes as they sat on the stand. These were the men and woman who were supposed to sit in judgment of me. It was obvious that they had already made up their minds, and this was before day one of my trial. The looks on their faces and the things they were saying, just added wood to the fire of anger that was raging in me. No matter what they said that day, no matter how tired I was when I returned back to the cell, I always made time to bend my knee in worship to Satan. The demonic presence began to get stronger as I continued to worship Satan. I'd have really strange dreams as I'd not only see many demons but also interact with them. After waking up from such nightmares, I would vividly remember the dream exactly as it had occurred. On such days, a demonic presence hovered around me for the rest of the day. Even my desires began to change and became evil in nature. I no longer just desired to get out of jail – I had a purpose that I wanted to fulfill upon getting out of jail and with my life. I desired to open a satanic church like no other and build Satan an altar where I could publicly practice sacrifices. The more Satan filled me with his lies and wickedness, the deeper I fell into depression and the worse my attitude became.

It took about two months for my jury selection to come to an end. We'd selected 12 jurors and two alternate jurors. We were ready for my trial to begin. I knew from the very beginning that these men and woman were not my peers. I'd grown up in a different world than them, yet they were not only going to sit in judgment of me, they were also going to weigh between a life or death sentence for my charges. My life was at their mercy!

I did find it funny that on questionnaires most of them had mentioned that they were Christians. I guess they must have been without sin because they were getting ready to cast several stones in my direction, until I was dead. Or maybe they had just missed or skipped that part of the bible.

Every night, I'd keep the blood pact that I'd written and signed with Satan under my mattress. During daytime, I had to keep it hidden as I have no doubt that it would have been used against me, had they found it. All the dreams and interactions I was having with demons were filled with specific images and promises. They were images of material wealth, power, and I even saw a specific design for a satanic church. These were all images of things I believe they were offering me if I continued to serve them. Yet, nowhere was the promise of freedom from my mental shackles of anger and depression. I now understand that there are many things that Satan can offer a person, but just as many that he cannot give. No matter what kind of promises he makes, he can never give you peace or joy in your life, as he cannot give away what he himself does not have.

CHAPTER 7:
"DEATH BY LETHAL INJECTION"

By the first day of my trial, I had already deteriorated mentally. While I was physically in the courtroom, my mind was somewhere very far away. During my time in prison, I have met with many prisoners who suffer from depression and other mental disorders. The results are always the same: They are kept medicated and in a zombie-like state. In my time here, I have also attempted to hold conversations with some of these men while they are on "medication." It is nearly impossible. They usually have the same look on their faces of not really knowing where they are. It feels as if they are staring straight through you, as if you are not even there.

I believe any kind of medication would have just made things worse for me. I don't believe I was expressing any kind of outward signs of my depression, other than maybe my attitude and my weight gain. I tried my hardest to always appear upbeat. I'd always be smiling and joking with my attorneys. Even though I was on trial for my life, many times my mind would just wander to other things. I couldn't seem to stay focused for long periods of time, and before I knew it the trial days had come and gone.

There were roughly 200-300 people in the courtroom when I walked in on the first day and none were there on my behalf. My family had not been allowed to be there due to a trick by the prosecution. Instead, my family was held in a room next to the actual courtroom as the trial moved forward. When I'd enter the courtroom, the air always seemed thicker than in other places. Whether that was because of the tension and hatred in the room, or the demons that I was bringing with me, I do not know.

When I would return to the cell, late in the evenings, the first thing I would do was bend my knee to worship Satan. The blood pact that I'd made with Satan always stayed near me when I prayed. One night, early in my trial, I fell asleep and I had a lucid dream or perhaps it was a vision. I had a dream or vision where I found myself getting out of jail as a free man. I then opened a satanic church, but this freedom I was seeing wasn't free, it came at a high cost, and the price was against my own mother and father.

Even with all the anger and hatred I had within me, I didn't believe I could ever bring any harm to my family. My family had nothing to do with what I was going through. They had been there for me from day one and were ready to help me at a moment's notice.

My trial was nothing but a big show for the audience. My attorneys, I now believe, had no intentions of really helping me. I believe they had sold me out before the trial had even begun. The prosecution should have won an Oscar for their performance as it was truly flawless. There were some days when all seemed to be going my way, and had my attorneys pushed forward and followed those leads, perhaps the trial would have gone my way. The state witnesses were confused in what they were saying, some of them in contradiction to themselves and others. I didn't even care if they gave me a life sentence without the possibility of parole, or if they gave me a death sentence. It was all the same to me: both meant death inside prison walls. I just wanted this to be done and over with.

I already knew I was going to be found guilty because my defense team didn't seem to put any effort into defending me thoroughly. My lead-attorney even told me, at one point, that it was not their job to prove my innocence, maybe in a perfect justice system that belief would have some merit, but not in the one of Texas where one must *prove* one's innocence beyond *all* doubt in order to be acquitted.

The case was finally handed over to the jury after about two weeks of testimony, argumentation, and presentation. Most of those two weeks had been spent by the prosecution presenting their side. When the jury took the case, I was moved to a holding cell next to the courtroom. My mind was a big blur from all the things I had running through my mind as I sat in the cell. My blood was boiling from everything I'd seen and heard. The acting and drama that the prosecution had presented had gotten to me. Seeing how the jurors ate up everything that was fed to them was extremely irritating to me. I had to sit there and watch everything, knowing that these men and woman were never my peers. They had not grown up in a place where law enforcement is corrupt. They couldn't even phantom the idea that the prosecution would lie or manipulate in order to get a conviction. While there are many men and women in both the justice system and law enforcement who have integrity, there are also many who have not. Some people will do anything in order to advance their careers, even if that means perverting justice from time to time.

The jury took several hours to deliberate before coming back with a decision. I was escorted back into the courtroom and afterwards the jury came in. I saw the faces of each individual juror as they took their seats. None of them would even look my way, except for one. She was a woman with blond hair in her late 40s or early 50s. This specific juror had stated in her voir dire that she had known the family of the victims for over 20 years. The fact that she was even on the jury says much about the justice system here in Texas. I can assure you that had someone known my family for 20 years and had attempted to be on my jury, they wouldn't have made it past the initial questionnaire. As the woman walked into the courtroom, she gave me a dead stare and wouldn't take her eyes of me. I obviously wasn't in the room while the jury discussed my case. However, if I had been a gambling man,

I'd confidently bet that this woman was a driving force in that jury room, not only in the innocence/guilt phase of the trial, but I'm sure it was no different during the punishment phase as well. That is human justice for us, or revenge rather said. Once the jury was seated, the judge asked the head juror if the jury had come to a decision. The head juror responded in the affirmative and handed a small piece of paper to the bailiff who then handed it to the judge. I sat there at the defense table and watched all this as if it was a perfectly choreographed act. The judge slowly and perfectly unfolded the piece of paper and read it to himself. He then said, "Will the defendant please rise." I found even the word "please" out of the judge's mouth to be funny. I rose from my seat and my attorneys did so too. In a strong and clear voice, the judge said, "In the charge of capital murder, the jury finds the defendant, Raul Cortez, guilty as charged." Now, why wasn't I surprised! Why wasn't I shocked and outraged! Perhaps it had something to do with the fact that I had attorneys who were determined to defend me to the least of their legal abilities, just enough to be able to say, "We did our job." Or perhaps it was because I'd known from the beginning of the trial that the jury members already had death in their hearts. Though I wasn't surprised, I was actually somewhat relieved as I was halfway done with the whole situation, and I knew that the end would come soon. I didn't care what the outcome would be since I knew it was either going to be life in prison or death – there wasn't any other option.

After the verdict was read, the court was adjourned for the day. The next phase, which was the punishment phase, was to begin the following day. I exited the courtroom and was again reshackled and returned to the county jail. Upon returning to the jail, I was ready to go back to the cell and go to sleep. It had been a long and really stressful day, but to my surprise, instead of being taken back to the cell, I was instead taken to the unit's infirmary. For the second time, I found myself under suicide watch. Like before, I was nowhere near suicidal. Maybe I had the feeling of wanting to hurt others, but not myself. At that moment, all I really wanted was just to lie down and get some sleep. To this day, I still don't understand how putting someone who is suicidal in an empty cell is supposed to help them mentally. I stared at the ceiling. I'd been locked away for about 18 months in what could be considered a concrete box. I didn't really want a life sentence. I knew that a life sentence was just more of the same thing I'd already endured for the last 18 months. I hated those suicide cells. My trial had been a rollercoaster ride with too many highs and lows to count. It had left me drained – mentally, emotionally, and physically. Little did I know that the punishment phase would be even more taxing than the trial had been. I finally fell asleep that night. I was awakened early in the morning to get ready to face another battle.

I've heard people talk about depression and its symptoms, but capturing the essence of depression with words escapes me. I believe that only a person who has been through it can truly understand the grip that it takes on one's life.

On the first day of the punishment phase, I was so stressed that I was unable to turn my head to the sides or bend and tie my shoelaces. I felt the weight of the world on my shoulders, and at the time I believed that weight alone would be enough to finish me off.

Day after day, I had to sit during the punishment phase and hear about how "horrible a person I was." At times, my mind would wander so far off that the day would pass me by without hearing a word of what was said. Perhaps it was just my internal defense system blocking off all the horrible things that were being said about me. There were other days where I was fully alert, but even those days were extremely hard on me. I had to sit and listen to people, some of whom claimed to once have been my friend, saying horrible things about me. Even after over a decade, I still don't know why my alleged friends said the things they said about me. It has crossed my mind that perhaps they believed they could make a name for themselves, as it was a high profile case. However, I believe it is revealing that a few years after arriving on death row, I received a letter from my former roommate. He'd been my roommate at the time that the murders had taken place. In his letter, he told me that he had been threatened by the district attorney's office. He was warned against helping me or else he would be charged with the same crimes as me. He did show up during my trial and was sworn in as a witness for the state. However, in the end, he never took the stand and my attorneys never questioned him. I do wonder how many others were threatened to either testify or not testify against me. I do find that to be an unfair practice in our justice system. If my lawyers had threatened a state witness and put pressure on them to either testify or not, they could have been charged with a felony punishable by 10 years in prison. Yet the state prosecutors get a pass.

The hardest part of the sentencing phase for me was having to watch as my family took the stand in my defense and pleaded for mercy for my life, but the jury had no mercy and they were full of vengeance in their hearts. My heart was broken to pieces as I watched my family in that situation. My attorneys and I had agreed that we would not put my family on the stand, but they had done it anyway behind my back. My mind had been so far gone that I had not even noticed that my family was actually on the stand testifying on my behalf. It finally hit me when one of my attorneys told me to look at my sister who was on the stand. When they were done testifying, and I realized what had just occurred, I turned and looked toward the jury and saw their unmoved faces. I saw their anger, and I could sense that there was murder in their hearts.

I understood it because I, too, had the same anger and feelings of murder. I wanted to inflict vengeance on all those who were in the courtroom that day.

The seeds of anger that Satan had planted were beginning to blossom. I etched the faces of the jurors deep into my mind and swore to myself to never forget them. The punishment phase lasted for a week. The case was then handed over to the jury. I was removed from the courtroom and had to wait in the holding cell. I sat inside it with my back against the hard concrete wall. I was so angry that I had a hard time breathing. My mind couldn't escape the images of my family sitting on the stand, fearful and hurt, and then I would see the faces of the jurors and my anger would spike. The waiting was driving me crazy! I knew this thing was just for show: my sentence was going to be death. Other than having my family testifying in my defense, my attorneys had presented nothing else. Nevertheless, there was one bright side to all of this: at any moment, the guards would arrive and escort me back into the courtroom, and then it would all be over. My life was in the hands of people who had no idea who I was.

The jury deliberated for about five to eight hours. When they finally came to get me, it was about 10 p.m. I entered the courtroom and took my seat. Then the jury was brought back into the courtroom. My sentence was written all over their faces. All the hatred and disgust that had built up in them toward me was perfectly visible. None would turn and look at me except for the blond juror who couldn't take her eyes of me. Our eyes met as she took her seat, and with me being a prideful man, I refused to let her think that I feared death. I stared her down as hard as she was trying to dominate me with her intense stare. It only ended when the court was resumed.

Again, the judge went through the whole act of asking the head juror if they'd come to a decision. The head juror said that they had and the judge was handed a piece of paper with the verdict. The judge then made a show of unfolding it and reading the decision to himself. He thanked the jury for their service and dismissed them. I guess the blond juror was not going to get the chance to see my reaction to the decision, as I'm sure she would have loved to. Instead, the jurors had to walk out of the courtroom. When they had left, the judge looked toward me and told me to rise. There was that word again, "please." I really don't know why hearing that word bothered me so much, perhaps it was the hypocrisy in it, after all, he was about to sentence me to death. I stood up with my attorneys. The courtroom was eerily quiet for a few seconds. Only the judge's voice could be heard, and it seemed as if only he was moving and everyone else was on their tippy toes in anticipation.

In the State of Texas, in order to give a person the death sentence, the jury has to answer three questions a certain way. The questions and format might have changed today. Back then, the first question was: Was there an intentional murder committed while in the act of committing a second felony? The second question was: Is there a probability that the defendant will be a future threat to society? With this question, I feel as if the court makes seers and fortune tellers of the jury. The third question was: Are there any mitigating factors that cause you to believe that the defendant deserves a life sentence instead of death? These questions have to be answered yes, yes, and no, in order for the sentence to be death.

As I stood in the courtroom, the judge didn't read each question individually; rather, he said that the jury had answered, "Yes," to the first question, "Yes," to the second question, and, "No," to the third question. The next thing I remember is that the judge looked up at me from the piece of paper in his hands. He looked me straight into the eyes, and said the words, "death by lethal injection." I heard and understood that loud and clear. When he said that our eyes locked for what felt like several minutes. Then I remember giving him a big and sincere smile of all things. At that moment, as I stood there, a man sentenced to death, a thought came into my mind. I thought about how, ever since my childhood, someone or another had been trying to kill me, and for some odd reason that thought made me smile.

I know that the newspapers reported that, at some point, during the stage at which the family of the victims testified as to the impact of the crime, I smirked at one of the family members as they read their impact statement to me. If this were true, then I deeply apologize. I was there physically, but my mind was so fogged that I couldn't fully comprehend everything that was going on around me. I only write this to explain my distorted mind during that time. Depression and satanic oppression are extremely powerful chains of bondage, but there exists only one who is more powerful than both depression and satanic oppression combined, and His name is Jesus Christ.

There is one other thing that occurred that night as the judge gave me a sentence of death. It was something that would have never crossed my mind. It was something that I didn't come to find out about until many years later. What occurred that night was that as the judge sat on his bench, giving me a death sentence, somewhere far away yet at the same time not so far away, there was one who was and is seated, not on a bench but on the throne of grace (Hebrews 4:16). He looked down from His throne, at this convicted capital murderer, a Satanist, a man who was covered in sin, and was considered by society to be one of the worst of the worst who wasn't even deserving of life. He looked at me lovingly and declared to God the Father that I was His. He had already paid for my sins through His death on the cross and resurrection. I heard His still voice say, "I am VICTORIOUS over death and while they may say death to you I proclaim life to you in abundance." Glory be to God Almighty!

After my sentence, I was taken back to the county jail and placed in the same suicide watch cell as before. From what I was told, anyone sentenced to life, death, or anything over 30 years is automatically put on suicide watch. I truly do not believe this is done for a person's own protection as they claim but as an added retaliation toward the convicted. The prison system has nothing to do with rehabilitation at this point, but is focused on punishment. I was nowhere near suicidal.

It was finally over. There would be no more court hearings and no more testimonies after 18 months of sitting in the county jail. I believed that at the very least, I knew what the outcome of the whole situation was. I did, however, find it a little ironic that they would place a person sentenced to death on suicide watch. I guess they didn't want to risk losing the "privilege" of executing someone.

I lay on the bunk that night a man sentenced to death. Yet I felt no stress anymore. I fell asleep immediately. I was exhausted from all the weeks of trial. I had a dream that night where I was told I would be going to a place where the word of God was not preached. The meaning of those words didn't really mean anything to me at first. I wasn't a preacher, and in fact I didn't want anything to do with God. What did I care if the word of God was preached or not. So I dismissed the dream as just that.

The next morning, I was awakened by two guards – apparently I had been wrong, it wasn't all over yet. I had a court hearing I had to attend that morning. I was so tired of hearings and didn't want to see another courtroom, but this wasn't an option for me. All I wanted was to get as far away from courtrooms and courthouses as I possibly could. I got up and got ready and was driven the short ride from the county jail to the courthouse. Everyone there had been waiting for me to arrive. The place was empty that morning, apart from my defense team, the prosecution, the judge, and a few other staff members. The purpose of the hearing was so I could be appointed an attorney to represent me on my direct appeal. The direct appeal is the first post-conviction appeal. Being new to the system, I agreed to have my lead-attorney appointed. They convinced me that he was the best man for the job, as he had sat through the whole trial. That sounded like a reasonable argument. However, if I had the chance to do it over, I would not have agreed. Since he was one of my trial attorneys, he would probably never raise an issue that implicated him in making a mistake. After the hearing, I was taken back to that dreadful suicide cell. The suicide cell is about 12 by 15 feet and is kept empty, except for a thin mattress that is thrown on top of a concrete slab about 15 inches high. There is absolutely no privacy whatsoever at any time, even when one is using the toilet. There are always nurses and other personnel coming and going at all hours of the day and night. To someone who is psychotic or is weak-minded it can be complete torture. By God's mercy, I was neither psychotic nor was I weak-minded, but I was fatigued. I wasted the day away just lying around as there was nothing else to do. The following morning, I was allowed to go to the shower at about 6 a.m. The shower relaxed me a little and made me feel much better. Perhaps it was just getting out of the cell even for just a few minutes that made me feel better, as I was not being allowed to go to recreational area – which is also known as the exercise area even though there is no equipment.

After my shower, on the way back to my cell, I noticed a phone on the wall. I asked the guard, who had been waiting for me outside the shower, if I was allowed to use the phone.

Surprisingly, he said, "Yes." It was still early, but I called my mother anyway. I was sure she would be happy to hear from me no matter what time it was. My mom quickly picked up the phone and accepted the charges. I tried to give her words of comfort telling her that everything would be okay, and that I was doing fine. She didn't know that I was being held on suicide watch and I didn't tell her. I believe that would have just added to her pain and stress.

I shared the dream I had with her about me going to a place where the word of God was not preached. She didn't say much about it, but she took it to heart more than I had at the moment. No one in my family knew that I'd been praying to Satan or that I'd made a blood pact with him. All they knew was that my attitude had changed for the worse. I hung up the phone with my mother that morning, and my heart felt heavy with sorrow for them. I knew that they were feeling much pain in their hearts, and that was extremely painful to me. I didn't really care much about the fact that they had given me a death sentence. I really didn't value my own life anymore. With all that had been said and done, I still loved my mother and my father and the whole family. After the phone call, I headed back toward the cell. To my surprise there were a deputy and a U.S. Marshal standing outside the cell. They told me to get my stuff ready because they were my ride to "the row." I guess someone really wanted me out of the county jail – because I had never seen anyone transferred to prison that quickly during my whole time there. Nonetheless, I was ready. At least, I'd be out of the suicide cell and around other prisoners. I didn't have anything to pack. All my property had been taken from me when I was put on suicide watch the day I was found guilty. I never learned what happened to the blood pact I'd written when the prison staff found it, which they must have.

I got dressed in a county jail one-piece jumper. I was shackled with the usual belly chain, leg irons, and handcuffs, and was escorted to the county jail's sally port. There I was placed in the back seat of a light brown Ford and we were finally on our way to Texas death row.

CHAPTER 8:
TEXAS DEATH ROW: MY NEW HOME

It's about a 3-4 hour drive from McKinney to the Joe Byrd Unit in Huntsville. The Joe Byrd Unit is a diagnostic unit and is only a stepping stone on the way to Texas death row. During those hours on my ride to the unit, I had a torrent of thoughts running through my head. Most of all, I was relieved, and I was beginning a new phase in my life. How long this phase would last, I had no idea. I attempted to prepare myself mentally for what was to come my way. For example, I knew that sooner or later I would have to get into a fight. Whether that was with just one person or a group of people didn't really matter to me. Growing up in Chicago, I'd been in many fights, sometimes they had been one on one, other times they had been all out riots.

I knew that I was extremely out of shape for someone my age. The arrest, isolation, trial, and depression had taken a major toll on my health.

I was trying to imagine what death row was going to be like. I would be surrounded by those individuals society considered to be the worst of the worst. I'd be surrounded by men who were considered so dangerous that society had deemed that they could not be rehabilitated and must be put to death. Now, I was considered to be one of these men. To prison standards, I figured I would be alright as I had been convicted of four counts of capital murder, and I didn't have a snitch jacket coming into prison. The media had covered my case and trial so well that if I had a snitch jacket, it would have been well known. My case also didn't have anything to do with kids or rape charges. All things considered, I figured there were going to be many who would have a harder time in prison than me. However, no matter what my case involved or didn't involve, I knew I would be tested one way or another at some point. I actually felt a little excited and anxious at the same time. I'd grown up watching all the old prison movies and that was what I had pictured in my mind. Although, I had already been wrong once when I'd arrived at the county jail, I didn't think I could be too far off with what I imagined death row to be. I understood that these men who I would be confronting were like me and had nothing to lose. We had already been sentenced to death, so no matter what we did they could not stack up any more time on our sentence. What more could they do to us?

When we arrived at the Joe Byrd Unit, I saw a flurry of activity: there were inmates everywhere, all dressed in prison whites. They all seemed busy working at different tasks, some were mowing lawns, others were washing the incoming transfer buses, while some did various kinds of work. One thing was for sure, none were just standing around idle. I asked the officers, who were escorting me, if this was death row? They said it wasn't, but that this was as far as they went. I was a bit confused by their statement. I just went with the flow as I'd find out in the next few minutes where I was.

We drove into the prison and I was eventually escorted by two sergeants to a huge building with several transfer cages. Each cage looked as if it could hold at the very least 100 men. Though I'm sure if they needed to, they could squeeze a lot more in it. I was directed into one of these cages all by myself. Across from the cage I was in, there were about 100 men who had just alighted from a transfer bus, popularly known as a "bluebird." They were being searched and processed into the system. I was given prison clothes which consisted of a white pair of pants and a short.sleeved pullover shirt. The two officers, who had transferred me from the county jail, handed over my custody to the Texas Department of Criminal Justice (TDCJ). As a part of the intake process, I had my head shaved and had new mugshots taken. They also took several pictures of my tattoos from different angles, examined them, and asked me lots of questions about them. It was obvious that they were gang tattoos – it wasn't like I was attempting to hide that information from them. Their job was to study gangs, so they knew exactly what it was that they were looking at as soon as they saw them.

They asked me who I ran with in prison. I thought that was a baseless question, as they had my file on hand and knew this was my first time in prison. I told them I didn't run with anyone in or out of prison. They continued to ask me questions about prison families (prison gangs), which I honestly knew nothing about. The gang systems in Chicago and Texas are worlds apart. I didn't even know what the names of the prison families were in Texas. After a while, I guess they either got tired or believed I really didn't know anything about the prison gangs in Texas or how they operated, so they just moved on.

They also examined my work history, my educational level, and my family including my grandfather who had died several years back. Then, lastly, they surveyed my mental state, presumably to detect possible indications of mental illness and suicidal ideations.

Mentally I felt fine. I was just ready to get to wherever it was I was going to get to. After several hours of examination, I was taken back to the transfer cage I had first been in. I waited for about another hour while a transfer team came to pick me up. There were busloads after busloads of men coming and going the whole time I was there. Finally a transfer van arrived. I wouldn't be getting on a bluebird since a personal escort had been sent to pick me up. I was again shackled with the usual hardware, including a belly chain, leg irons, and handcuffs, but they also placed a small metal box over the center of the handcuffs and then secured it in place with a small master lock. I was then directed to the back of a white cargo van that had been fitted with individual cages inside. When I was inside the van, I thought it was funny that they put another master lock on my cage. Talk about security. There were three transfer officers in the van with me, and they were all armed to the teeth. There was at least one shotgun and several automatic pistols. As we were driving, I looked out of the back window and carefully observed the trees and the forest-like scenery as we went. It would be a long time before I saw this kind of scenery again, so I took it all in.

We drove for about one hour when we finally came to a large compound in the middle of nowhere. The Polunsky Unit is a huge, white building. From what I could see, there were many slits cut into the sides of the walls. For someone like me who had never been in prison before, it was a very imposing building. We went through a number of check points and were then directed to the back of the unit. After going through a number of gates, we arrived at a sally port. I had finally arrived on Texas death row.

CHAPTER 9:
"I CAN MAKE YOUR LIFE A LIVING HELL"

I was escorted into building number 12 where death row inmates are housed. This building is considered to be the highest security building in the TDCJ. I was escorted by the transfer officers down a long hallway to a small booth. They removed all the chains and shackles, which belonged to the transfer team, and then they went on their way as their job was done: I'd been securely transferred to death row. There were two sergeants standing there when the shackles were removed. I was again searched and given death row clothing, which consisted of a one piece jumper with the letters "DR" spray painted on one leg and on the back side of the jumper. After getting dressed, I was handcuffed with my hands behind my back.

I also had to go through their intake process, although this one was not as in-depth as it had been at the Joe Byrd Unit. I was first taken to the medical department or section where my vitals were taken. From here, I was brought to the small booth where a psychologist was waiting for me. She asked me a few questions about my mental state and if I had any known psychiatric disorders. I didn't. I'd only been to a hospital once when I had gotten shot several years ago. I asked her some questions about the living conditions on death row, and not surprisingly she was of no help. From there, I was taken to the classifications department. While there, I was asked if I had any enemies that I knew of. The only real enemy that came to my mind at that moment was them. They were the ones who wanted to kill me, but I didn't tell them that, of course. One of the sergeants, who had been escorting me, asked me out of nowhere, "Are you going to give us a hard time?" I didn't respond and gave him a stare. Was it starting already? Was I going to be tested even before I got to a pod? And by a sergeant for that matter! When he saw that I didn't answer him, he then said, "I can make your life a living hell back here." I just laughed at those words. The way I saw it, I could do the same and probably much worse. I wasn't the one who had to go home every day. However, I just held my tongue for the moment. After answering a few more questions, I was escorted down a long hallway to the C-pod. As we walked, I had a sergeant on each side of me. The one who had told me he could make my life a living hell, was holding me by my left arm. The second sergeant was a few steps behind us. I didn't feel comfortable walking with them with my hands cuffed behind my back. I took each step carefully expecting at any second to be slammed to the ground, but it never came.

I was assigned to the C-pod, cell number 56. Upon entering the pod, the first thing I noticed was the darkness, though it was the middle of the day and the sun was brightly shining outside. Building 12 consists of six pods – A through F, and each one has six sections. Each section has 14 cells, seven on each row. There is also a shower at the end of every run and a recreational area, which measures about 30 by 25 feet. It is closed in by prison bars, making it look like a huge cage. Lastly, there are two outside recreational yards on each side of the pod.

The first thing that I saw when I walked into the C-pod was a black inmate inside the F-section's recreational area. I didn't see anyone else with him, but I didn't think much about it at the moment. As we walked toward the D-section, where my cell was located, we passed by two other recreational areas. Interestingly, only one inmate was in each of them. I figured that these inmates might have requested to be alone. Personally, I'd just spent the last year and a half by myself, and I was definitely eager to be around other people. It hadn't hit me yet that death row inmates were held in isolation. I was alert as I walked toward cell 56, and I noticed that when the gates clanked open for the D-section many inmates came to the cell doors to see who had arrived. We walked up the stairs to the second row where cell 56 was located. The cell door was rolled open and I stepped inside. The sergeant opened a slot on the lower part of the cell door. I stuck my hands out through the slot, and he removed the handcuffs. I took a step forward and looked around the empty cell. The paint on the walls was chipped away, revealing the hard concrete behind. I saw my bed, if you can call it that as it was just a metal bunk. Three of the walls were made of concrete while one was made of stainless steel. A toilet sink combo was welded onto it. The cell was a perfect description of how I was feeling inside. My emotions had all been chipped away. The only thing that remained of me was a heart empty of all love and affection and as hard as the metal bunk I was looking at. If this was to be my life then so be it, I thought to myself. I would embrace it and become one with the hard cell. I stood in the middle of the cell and just looked around it for a few minutes. A new weight was beginning to bear down on me. I was through with my trial and the punishment phase and had felt some relief. However, death was now in sight.

I sat on the bunk with my back against the wall and let my mind run free for some minutes. I couldn't believe I was on Texas death row! I sat there lost in my own thoughts when I heard someone calling out, "Cortez! Look out Cortez!" I didn't move off the bunk as I was sure they were not calling me. I'd just arrived few minutes ago. A few seconds later I heard it again, "Cortez! Look out Cortez!" I still didn't move off the bunk since I had no interest in who this other Cortez was. Then they changed tactics and started calling out, "Look out cell 56!" I knew I was in cell 56 because I had seen the big numbers on the cell door when I was brought in. Cell 56 is a corner cell, so I only had one neighbor to my right.

My neighbor began to bang on the wall between the cells. He, too, began to shout my name. I finally got up and went to the cell door and said, "What's up?" He asked me if I had just arrived on the row. Before I answered him, I remember thinking to myself, "Okay, if this is where it is going to start, it might as well begin." With a bit of an attitude I responded to him, "Yea I just got here, why, what's up?" He then asked me if my name was Cortez. I said, "Yea my name is Cortez, who are you?" I remember thinking about in what way he apparently knew me. Then I thought that perhaps he was related to my co-defendant or to my case somehow. I told myself that I'd have to keep an eye out for him. He then told me that someone in the recreational area was trying to get my attention. I noticed a young guy there. He saw me standing at the door and asked me if my name was Cortez. I told him that's right. He then asked me if I had a nickname I went by, and I told him I didn't. When I was a kid growing up in Chicago, I went by the name Spooky or just Spook. However, more than a decade had passed and I wasn't going to go back to childish nicknames. He then surprised me by telling me that he had some stuff for me. He showed me a brown paper sack full of something. I silently laughed to myself at that – "He must think I'm one of these suburban kids who know no better." I told him that the stuff wasn't mine because I had just arrived. He then told me that he knew all that, but someone from a different section had said that he knew me. I was starting to get annoyed and told him, "Listen man, I ain't from Texas so anyone over there or anywhere else knows who I am! Send that stuff back to wherever it came from, I ain't interested." It wasn't that I was paranoid, I just felt really uncomfortable with all these people knowing who I was. The guy smiled and laughed to himself, and that really annoyed me. I thought he was laughing at me, rather than the situation. My neighbor heard the exchange and introduced himself to me as J.J. He explained to me that on Texas death row they have had a decade's long tradition. Whenever someone new arrives on death row, everyone pitches in whatever they can whether it is soups, soap, toothpaste, toothbrush, writing materials, or even clothing. They get everything together as a kind of care pack for the person, not expecting anything in return. Everyone knows that when someone arrives on the row, they arrive without any property. Everyone here has been through this at least once upon arrival. It can sometimes take a couple of months before an ID is issued, which is required for you to purchase commissary. That is, if you have money to purchase any.

Here I was, a stranger on Texas death row, and my first experience with those who are considered by society to be evil, dangerous maniacs was love and kindness. J.J. explained to me that nobody wanted any of this stuff back. I knew that the first rule of prison life is to never take anything from anyone you don't know because nothing is free in prison. He, however, explained to me that the same thing had been done for the men who were here presently. He also told me that if I ever found myself in a position to help someone who had just arrived, then I should do the same for them. After telling me that, he sent a homemade line through a hole at the bottom of the cell door with a bottle of water attached to the end as a weight. The bottle went sliding across the run until it reached the recreational area, which was about 50 feet away. This I later learned was called "fishing." When the "fishing line" made it to the area, the young inmate climbed about 10 feet of prison bars until he was on the second row and tied the bag on the end of J.J.'s line. J.J. then pulled the line to the cell door and slid it in front of the cell I was in. The whole thing took about 30 seconds from start to finish.

J.J also clarified to me that we were kept in what is called "AD-SEG," which is administrative segregation. What that meant was that I was being held in isolation. While he was talking to me, all I could think about was isolation. He told me that we were basically kept in solitary confinement at all times, even if it was called by a different name. We were allowed exercise time in the recreational cage for two hours per day, but only for five days per week. We also had single man cells, and thank God we also had single man-showers! We were standing at the door talking for a while when I finally asked him how he knew my name. He told me that everyone sentenced to death is held at the Polunsky unit, so they had already been expecting me when I'd gotten sentenced. My name had been mentioned over and over again in the newspapers and on the radio.

As we were talking, a guard passed by and saw the brown bag in front of the cell door. I wasn't going to ask the guard for anything. The way I saw things, they were the enemy, but J.J. talked to the guard and told him that I had just arrived on the row and asked him if he could help me get the bag in the cell. The guards were well aware that the practice of care packs took place. Most of them had no problem with it. Neither did they have a problem assisting people get stuff moved around. The guard told me to take a step back, away from the cell door. He rolled the cell door open and placed the bag inside the cell, no handcuffs, no shackles, no nothing. I looked inside the bag and I was grateful for the kindness the men had shown me. I didn't care much about the food that was in the bag. What was really important was the hygiene- and writing materials.

I was dying to make a phone call, but I was unaware that they were not allowed. I knew my family still had no idea that I had been transferred. I had just spoken to my mother from the county jail when they had arrived to pick me up.

Later that day in the evening, the guards came around, passing out lunch trays. My first tray on death row consisted of chili mac and some brown vegetables with a piece of cornbread. I placed the tray on the small table/shelf in the cell, and only then realized I didn't have a spoon or a fork, and I was really hungry! Not thinking twice about it, I got up, washed my hands, and sat back down on the bunk. Hungrily, I looked at the chili mac and dug in with my bare hands. A guard passed by and saw me eating this way. By now, my chin was covered in chili mac sauce. He just looked at me and moved on. On that first night on death row, I had no mattress in the cell to lie on. I only had a thin sheet as a cushion between me and the bunk.

I had spent the last year and a half in the county jail where the inmates have no control of the cell lights during the day or night. In the county jail, the lights are controlled by an officer. During the night, the main lights are turned off but a nightlight is left on. When I got tired the first night, I went to bed with the big cell light on. I couldn't sleep. It wasn't only because of the hard bunk, but also because of the bright cell light that was still on. I kept tossing and turning trying to find a comfortable position to no avail. When breakfast was served, I still had not been able to fall asleep. I asked the guard who was passing out the breakfast trays when they would be turning off the cell lights. She gave me a strange look and asked me if the light button didn't work in the cell. I turned and looked at the button that was on the stainless steel wall and just laughed at myself. I told her I didn't want breakfast and finally turned off the light and fell into a restless sleep. Later that morning, J.J. asked me if I had gotten the light to go off. I told him that I just didn't know it was a light button. I thought that it was an intercom button in case I was choking on a chicken bone or something and needed help. Immediately, J.J. bust out laughing, and said, "Bro if you are choking on a chicken bone, then you need to learn to give yourself the Heimlich maneuver! Because these people working back here couldn't care any less what happens to you or me. The way they see it, it's just one less person they have to feed and execute." Those were harsh words, but very true. When I woke up, I went to the shower area and skipped going for exercise. Any time we left the cell, or any other place, we always had to be handcuffed with our hands behind our backs. When I stepped out of the cell, I could hear that someone was singing a Christian song. When I passed the man's cell, it was obvious that he was singing as loudly as he could. The funny thing was that he was completely naked! I quickly turned away and continued to walk toward the shower area, which was at the end of the run. At the same time, I noticed that an inmate was outside exercising. He was running around in circles. As he ran, he was attempting to outsing the man who was singing in his cell. I felt as if I had ended up in a nuthouse rather than death row. Within the first day and a half, I had been able to see genuine kindness of strangers, but I had also observed the insanity that comes from being housed in long term isolation. It was an extremely eye opening experience for me.

The following day, I figured I'd better go to the recreational area to get some exercise and to find out more about how things worked on the row. I also wanted to say thanks to the men who had sent me the items. The only problem was that I didn't know any of them, except one who had sent me a kite with the items. A kite is a message written by an inmate to another. He had told me in the kite that if I needed anything to let him know. The next day, I went to the section he was housed at, and it turned out that I did know who he was, though not personally. I recognized him right away since I'd seen him on TV. He'd had a really high profile case as well. He'd been involved in car chase that I had watched live on TV. He went by the nickname, Pitbull. To this day, he has been a good friend.

Inmates were not always taken to the same recreational cage, so we had the opportunity to become acquainted with other inmates. One day, I was exercising in the F-section when someone asked me if I could help him pass something to another section. This is the way we get things moved around on the row. A package sometimes has to pass through six inmates or more, before it can get to the intended person. I agreed to assist him and he sent his fishing line to my cage, and I took the stuff off his line, and passed it over to the E-section. After I passed the stuff, the same inmate asked me in Spanish if I wanted some *warinche*. Red with rage, I turned and looked at him with a clenched fist and responded scornfully by asking him if he wanted some warinche! He smiled not knowing why I had suddenly gotten mad. He replied, "Oh you already had some?" I had absolutely no idea what warinche was. It just didn't sound right to me. I asked him what he was talking about, and he laughed like never before and told me that it is slang for coffee in prison. I couldn't help it and had a great laugh, too. This was just one example out of many of how I had to learn new words that had completely different meanings from their original. I believe that some of the words, like warinche, are just made up, but then there are other words and terms, like *la playa* which literally means, the beach, but on the row it means, the shower. Or how about, *dale mariao*, which in English means, play it dizzy, which is used to tell someone to hold up a minute. *Cacawates*, which is peanuts in Spanish, means, pills, on the row. These were just a few of the words, I would have to quickly learn and get used to.

I didn't stay in cell 56 for very long. About three weeks after arriving on the row, I was sent back to the county jail due to a hearing. My attorney told me that it was all just for show and a waste of time and tax payer money. The next day, I was sent back to death row. Unfortunately, I had to go through the Joe

Byrd Unit first, although this time it was nowhere near as intense as the first time had been. I was in and out of the unit in less than an hour. I hated the ride to the Polunsky Unit. The road frequently curves and the transfer team drive really fast as they do not have to abide by the speed limits. After being in a stable cell for so long, I would get motion sickness from riding in a vehicle.

I arrived back on the row and after about 10 minutes of formalities, I wasn't taken back to my usual cell, but to cell 40 in the D-pod, my new home. I was lucky enough to be housed with good neighbors on either side of me. I quickly learned that just having good neighbors is a blessing in itself. Good neighbors can sometimes determine how easy or hard your time is going to be. In this aspect, I guess it is not much different from the free world.

My neighbor on my left was a really smart guy when it came to law. He often attempted to help me with my appeals, but I was really not interested. I had been drained of all motivation, and I didn't care about my appeals. He had already been on death row for well over two decades. Sadly, he died in 2017 of colon cancer. It was a hard thing to watch as the cancer ate at him until he was mere bones. My other neighbor to the right was a Hispanic guy named Frankie. We became really good friends throughout the years. He had already spent a decade on the row, and when I met Frankie in 2009, he had already run through all of his appeals and had been expecting an execution date. He did receive one several years later. He showed me who was who when it came to the different prison families, but I wasn't really interested in any of that, though it was good information to know. I was more interested in the fact that he knew how to make hooch (prison wine).

My feelings of despair, emptiness, and darkness continued to grow every day. The anger inside me – I held onto it with all the strength I had. Satan had convinced me that my anger was normal. I continued to believe that I had a right to feel this way. After all, I was sitting in a cell on Texas death row. I believed it was the one thing that was giving me strength to wake up every morning and get off the bunk. I wanted revenge. I wanted to hurt those who I felt had wronged me. I could clearly remember the faces of all those who had sat in the courtroom with me during my trial, especially their reactions and expressions when my family had asked for mercy. I truly believed that every one of those persons were my enemies.

Frankie and I had grown up in very different places, though not in very different ways. There was a hole in the wall between the cells we were in, and we used that one to communicate through. One day, as we were talking, he was telling me a story about a time when he got drunk in the exercise area, and ended up being sent to the F-pod – which is the disciplinary pod. I was very interested in how he made alcohol, and Frankie was eager to share his knowledge.

The readers may have heard that hooch is made in toilets, but I can assure you that it is not. Frankie then broke down the process for me and outlined the things I would need to buy, and it sounded quite easy. By this time, I had already been on the row for a couple of months and had purchased commissary a few times. As soon as I could, I bought everything I needed. There was no way of knowing how this small decision would change my life forever. After buying everything I needed, I was really excited for the first time since my arrest. Frankie offered to make the first batch for me and keep it in his cell while it cooked. Prison hooch takes a minimum of five days to make due to the fermentation process, and the longer it is left to ferment the stronger it gets. The first batch was left to ferment for five days, and I couldn't wait! We'd made plans to drink on the following weekend, and when the weekend finally arrived I was ready! That

Saturday evening, Frankie sent me three water bottles full of hooch. Empty water bottles or empty potato chip bags were used to both cook and transport the hooch. I didn't have a radio at the time because they had been sold out for several months. Fortunately, Frankie did have one and through some cutting and altering of a second pair of head phones, I was able to listen to Frankie's radio by touching the bare ends of the headphone cord to either the table/shelf or the metal bunk. It is truly amazing the things that these men come up with when the need arises. So I was set for the weekend: I had three bottles of hooch, plenty of snacks, and a means to listen to music while I drank and got drunk.

CHAPTER 10:
WHAT IS TRUTH?

I remember opening the first bottle and taking a sniff. The smell of alcohol hit me immediately and gave me goose bumps. My body was completely clean of all drugs and alcohol. I hadn't even taken a non-aspirin in over a year and a half. I took my first swig and felt a warm feeling that traveled from the top of my head and all the way down to my toes. The taste was horrible! However, the feeling I had felt from that first swig was incredible. I drank the three bottles throughout the night, as I listened to music and talked to Frankie through the hole in the wall. I'd found what I'd been looking for. The hooch had dissipated my anger and all negative feelings I had. I'd finally found solace. I'd found a cure for the battle that was brewing in me. I finally passed out in the wee hours of the morning. I woke up sometime around noon with a hangover like never before.

While in the free world, I'd spent many days on drinking binges, but I had never had a hangover like this before. Nevertheless, the hangover didn't matter to me, as I'd get used to them with time. I'd found what was going to help me get through my time on Texas death row. I quickly learned how to make it for myself. I didn't want to be dependent on anyone for my own fix. Seeing that hooch took anywhere from 5-7 days to properly cook, I was going to have to find a way to cook plenty of it while finding a way to hide it and masking its smell during fermentation. It is against prison rules to make hooch and our cells are claustrophobically small.

I figured out that the best way to hide the hooch was by placing it at the back of my locker and move my property in front of it. I covered up the smell by placing cologne sample strips on the air vents. At first, I started drinking just a few bottles on the weekends. Gradually, the amount began to increase as the weeks rolled by. It quickly went from just on the weekends to every couple of days. Before I knew it, I was drinking just about every day. I justified it by telling myself that there was no reason for me to deny myself simple pleasures. I felt great when I was drunk. I hated the hangovers, but I was slowly getting used to them. My tolerance began to increase the more I drank. It seemed as if I needed more and more every time to reach the same level of intoxication. I got to the point where I was cooking hooch inside big trash bags. After a while, I stopped caring about trying to hide the hooch, or even attempting to cover the smell. If the guards walked in the cell they were going to both see it and smell it. There was not much I could really do about it. They did walk into my cell on many occasions, yet they never made a big deal about it. Perhaps, they, too, were struggling with alcohol and could relate to my alcoholism. Or, perhaps, they left me alone because I was keeping to myself and did not cause them any trouble, even when I was drunk. Or just maybe, it was Satan that was blinding them to what was in front of them.

Several months went by, and the hooch finally stopped having the same effect on me that it'd had in the beginning. I attempted to make it stronger, but it didn't work. It seemed as if I had lost my cure. A friend of mine then introduced me to pill popping. I'd never really been into prescription medicine when I was free. I'd taken Xanax bars before, but all they had done was putting me to sleep. I'd usually take them when I was coming down off other drugs, just so I could fall asleep. I began by taking one Benadryl, which is the most available medicine on death row. I'd take one with a few bottles, and I found that it did increase my level of intoxication. I no longer needed as many bottles to get drunk, but just like with the alcohol my tolerance would quickly increase. Soon I'd be taking anywhere from 10-15 pills at once while continuing to drink hooch.

Then there were some days when hooch was not available to me. Sometimes the commissary was out of an ingredient I needed, or I would have consumed it all before the next batch was ready. Juice is a must have when making hooch on the row. We are limited to just one case of juice every two weeks. I began to ask my friends to buy me a case of juice on their accounts. I would in turn get them whatever they wanted on my own account. On the days when I didn't have hooch available, my depression would hit me the hardest. I self-medicated by spending my days drugged out on Benadryls, lying on the bunk, eating and reading, or listening to the radio all day long. As all addicts know, when your fix is gone your emotions fly high. I found myself to be quick tempered and frequently irritated during dry days. Every little thing would get under my skin and begin to annoy me. The Benadryls, too, would give me a kind of hangover. They would make me feel really heavy and groggy the next day. I spent many days and nights drunk and plotting in my mind the things I would do to certain people if I ever had the opportunity. Anger and hatred had grown like a vine around my heart, and as it squeezed my heart it sent fantasies of violence to my mind.

I was only in my late twenties and yet my health had rapidly deteriorated. I had gained lots of unhealthy weight and was gaining even more. Lying around the cell all day long wasn't helping me at all. Although I was always either high on pills or drunk, I still found myself with too much time on my hands – I was locked in a cage 22 hours per day for 5 days a week, and 24 hours two days per week. The alcohol was giving me what I believed was an escape from reality. Little did I know that the pills and alcohol were placing me in their own mental and physical prisons. Like any other "quick fix," it was never enough and it never lasted. It would feel good for a while, but I always needed more and more to reach the level where I felt sufficiently detached from my reality.

One day I was staring at the ceiling when a thought occurred to me. I was going to do something with all the time I had on my hands. I wanted to find "truth," and I considered the difficult question, "Does objective truth really exist?" When Jesus Christ was before Pontius Pilate, he asked Jesus, "What is truth?" (John 18:38). That was the same question I wanted an answer to. What *is* truth, where could I find the meaning of truth? Was truth just what I believed? Was it the same for all, or could there be variation of truths? For some reason, I was suddenly eager to investigate, read, and engage my mind. I no longer wanted to just waste away my days lying on the metal bunk.

I connected truth with religion for some reason, believing the two were interconnected. However, my premise just brought me more questions than answers: Which religion was true? Was there really just one true religion? Was there really just one belief system that could lead everyone to the truth? If there was just one true religion, what of the billions of good people who believed in a wrong ideology? Were they really doomed because of that? I began to study a few of the major religions of the world. I knew that I obviously could never study all religions in depth. I reasoned that if truth was actually real and could be found in religion, it would stand out from the rest. I began reading books on Buddhism, Hinduism, the Cabbala, Gnosticism, Islam, and even dived into various philosophical teachings. It never crossed my mind to seek truth in Jesus Christ. I wanted nothing to do with Jesus Christ or Christianity. For some reason, I felt great hatred toward the two. Maybe it was that I felt I had already given Christ and Christianity a chance, yet I still found myself on Texas death row.

Upon my arrival on death row, there were some inmates who attempted to talk to me about Christ, but they were ill prepared. Perhaps it was the demon who I already had inside of me or just my way of thinking. When these preachers approached me, I would manipulate the Bible to my advantage, and many times I'd leave them feeling embarrassed and ashamed. After that, they would never try to win my soul for Christ again. I actually felt good at putting them to shame. In retrospect, I was able to win the argument due to their knowledge of scripture being weak. After months of poring over dozens of books on many religions, I came across one called *The Book of Enoch*. I found it to be different than the rest of the books I'd read. The Bible tells us that "Enoch walked with God and was not there because God took him" (Genesis 5:24, HCSB). The book of Enoch is also quoted in Jude verse 14. So there is no doubt that Enoch was a man of God.

For some reason this book sparked something inside of me that no other book or study had been able to do. While studying Buddhism, I learned about "A Way to Nirvana." That way is reached by disposing oneself of all human desires from one's life. This includes even one's own family and loved ones. It isn't Buddha who delivers you to Nirvana, but it is his "Noble Truths" that instruct you to the way. In Hinduism, I learned that they have well over 1000 gods, and that a person who dies comes back to life through reincarnation. Yet, I also learned that they believe in what they call the "first birth." The first birth is when a person is first introduced into this world. However, Buddhism, in my opinion, fails to account for the flowing question: "Who sinned or what wrong was done so that one must suffer during that first life?"

When a person is reincarnated, he may come back as an animal or a bug. Not only was this unappealing but it also didn't have the sound of truth to me.

I then studied Islam, and found that in Islam it was all about submission to the Koran and to Sharia law. What I learned from Islam is that no matter how rigorously a person may follow the Koran, you are never guaranteed acceptance into heaven, unless you are killed in a Jihad, which means, holy war. Furthermore, it is not Mohammed who transforms you, but the Koran. Day after day, I would pour over religious texts seeking truth but coming out even more lost than when I had started.

I later studied Gnosticism and found that it was a mixture of Greek philosophy and Pagan religions. I found the Kabbala somewhat interesting, but it, too, was just a mixture of philosophy and symbolic interpretations of scriptures. None of these religions had any sound of truth to me. I was obviously unable to get into the heart and depth of each of these religions, and I'm sure there is much I don't know about them. Although, I didn't know what truth was or what exactly it was that I was looking for, I felt I wouldn't find it in these religions.

The book of Enoch was still on my mind as it had done something to me. At the very least, I had found it interesting more than I could say about the other books I had read. That might have been because I had grown up in the church, and Enoch was a Bible character. I was reading everything I could get my hands on that had something to do with religion. I was earnestly seeking truth no matter where it led me. One day, a friend of mine told me that we could order books ourselves without having to have them sent in by friends or family. He sent me a catalog from a company that sold all kinds of occult books and paraphernalia. I knew that I could never ask my family to send me such books. Whether they were strong Christians or not didn't matter, we'd grown up in a Christian home knowing that once a door was cracked open to the occult, it would quickly be wide. My family had no idea what I was doing behind these walls. As I looked through the catalog I saw many titles that sounded interesting. Not all of them had the occultist titles one would imagine. Many of them had completely innocent sounding titles, especially the self-help books. In retrospect, Satan does not always appear to people in a red suit with horns while holding a pitchfork. Usually, he will appeal to people in a very desirable way. I found a book in the catalog which shared title with another character from the Bible, but it didn't sound like a Christian book. I ordered the book and several weeks later it arrived. I began to read it and couldn't put it down from page one. It was like no other book I had ever read. It was full of "spells" that had been written by King Solomon according to the book. I didn't believe I'd found truth in what I was reading, but I did believe that what I was reading was true, if that makes any sense. When I had finished the book I was a bit disappointed. While it was full of "magic spells," it only had "white magic" spells. Today, after much studying of the Bible, I know that there is no difference between white magic and black magic or any other color as it is an abomination to the one True God, as it is stated in Leviticus chapter 18.

There are many men behind these death row walls who study and practice everything from Paganism, Santeria, Satanism, Voodoo, to many other occult practices. Due to this, it was very easy for Satan to put whatever he wanted into my hands. The more I began to read about the occult, the more I began to open myself up to it and everything that comes along with it. I began to practice small rituals as I was learning the meaning of the different symbols and prayers. I found myself drawn to black magic more than any other practice, along with its blood rituals. I ordered a few items like parchment paper, different prayer books, an alter cloth, and lots of other books. I began to practice more rituals as I was learning them, while continuing to feed my mind as much as I could. I learned how to summon demons and the difference between an invocation and an evocation. At first, I wholeheartedly didn't believe any of it, but in reality every time I performed an invocation, I was inviting legions of demons. These demons would remain quiet as they demolished me from the inside out. I was preparing myself for a major fall, but I was blind to it. I went on this way for many months. Time continued to sweep by me unnoticed while my rage and anger continued to burn. I didn't take it out on the people around me. Instead, I believe I was taking it out on myself through self-destruction, such as by cutting myself. I've known several people who have self-mutilated. They all did it for their own reasons. I am not exactly sure what it is that drives a person to want to cut themselves, or whether there are different degrees of this illness. I know that the reason I was cutting myself was because the books I was reading said that blood was required in order to perform some of the rituals, just as other rituals required fire and the burning of candles or parchment paper. Fire was not hard to obtain in the cell as I would use two pieces of pencil lead to pop up the electrical circuit and get a spark. I'd use cotton from medicine bottles as tinder and then get a small flame going. The candles were easy to make. I'd use petroleum jelly and roll up strings of cotton with some wire mixed into the string as a wick.

The blood, though, was difficult for me. I'd never cut myself before and to be honest I was scared the first time. In the county jail, I'd poked myself on the fingertip enough so that I bled just enough to write my pact, but at this point I was actually thinking about putting an actual razor to my finger tip and slicing myself. The first time I attempted it, I had taken a blade out of a double bladed razor which was given to us every week for shaving. The blade wasn't new, but I believed it was still sharp enough to cut me without much effort. I put the razor to the tip of my index finger of my left hand and just held it there. I was attempting to build up the courage to jerk my hand down and cut myself. It takes a lot more courage to than one might think. I had a girlfriend many years ago who was a self-mutilator. She had done it for so many years that she would do it with such an ease, and from years of self-abuse her arms were covered in scars all over. She suffered from depression and bi-polar disorder, and I believe that cutting herself relieved her from pain induced by the mental illnesses.

I also had another friend who would cut himself, but he would cut himself on his feet. Then he would go outside and rub his feet on the grass and dirt. I asked him why he did it, and he told me that when he was young, his mother had gotten an infection that had begun on her feet. The infection began to grow until the doctors were forced to amputate – she ended up losing both her feet all the way to the hips. My friend was mad that it had happened to his mother, and he wanted the same infection his mother had gotten. As for me, I didn't want to hurt myself in any way. I'd been shot before, and I just didn't like the sight of my own blood outside of my body. It took a while, but I finally built up the courage and just moved my right hand with the blade quickly across my finger. I gave myself a good scratch, but had not pierced through the skin. I did it again – this time I applied pressure as I ran the blade across my finger, and my finger gushed blood, perhaps a little bit more than what I needed. Without question, I was really heading down a dark and lonely road.

CHAPTER 11:
A SPIRITUAL BATTLE

May our Lord continue to bless my family today and always. They have been a pillar for me even in the darkest of times. Through it all, they have continued to stand by my side, never dropping their banner of faith in Jesus Christ even though they were just as burdened as I was. They continued to faithfully take that four hour drive each way, two to three times every month to just have a two-hour visit with me through a plexiglas, and I am sure that if I were allowed more visits per week they would have been there. During our visits, I'd attempt to hide everything about the life I was living. I figured the less they knew, the better off they would be. I'd always go to the visitation area with a fake smile on my face. However, can a son really hide anything from the mother who gave birth to him? Can a son really hide anything from the eyes of a father who has held and loved him since birth? I don't believe it can be done. I did my best, but obviously my mom and dad knew that something wasn't right – even my accelerating weight gain would have been a potent clue to my psychological health. They probably reasoned that it was due to the stress of the sentence that I carried and to a certain point I guess that was true, but the majority of it was due to my own doing. As the loving parents that they are, they continued to talk to me about Christ and His love for me. It didn't affect me at all. It would go into one ear and right out of the other. I was more concerned about the bottles of hooch I was going to drink the second I got back to the cell. On visitation days, I'd have to go easy on the bottles and pills. I loved my parents and I didn't want to disrespect them by going out there so high or drunk that it was obvious that I was on something. I understood that it was a big sacrifice on their part to drive all that way just to see me, not to mention the cost associated with the trip. By this time, there were only two people in my family who were aware that I had begun to experiment with the occult. I'd withheld that from my parents because I truly believed, had they known how deep I had gone into the abyss, it would have literally given them a heart attack.

My mother and father were persistent in their prayers for me, and just like when I was a teenager, they would spend whole nights with no sleep and on their knees praying for me. They continued even while I was on death row, and I believe that God was not only seeing their every tear drop, but answering their every request. I just didn't see the spiritual battle that was being fought in the heavens and all around me. My mind had been made cloudy by all the hooch and prescription drugs. I could no longer sleep without self-medicating. My body needed something to appear 'normal' to those around me. I needed more and more as my body was quickly adapting to the hooch and the Benadryl. By now, I had gone from taking one Benadryl to taking handfuls with my drinks. Yet they were no longer having the same effect. I therefore began to feel the symptoms of depression creep into my life again. The drugs and alcohol had never solved my problem of depression. They had just been a method of covering up the problem temporally and allowing me to forget about it for a while, just like the quiet demons that were just lying in my heart preparing to strike me when the time was right.

I still hadn't recognized the symptoms of depression. I only knew that I found myself more and more tired, always frustrated, and irked by every little thing. I hated the world and everyone in it. I began to experiment with different kinds of pills from Zoloft to Thorazine and Proxin. It didn't really matter to me if I took them together or separately. I just needed something in my system to make me numb to the world around me. All I wanted was peace, but peace was elusive. The weeks had become months and now about a year and a half had passed. It was August 2010 and I was in the fourth cell since arriving on Texas death row. I'd spent the first year and a half intoxicated. Other than getting high, the only other thing I did was read books on the occult. I had given up on my search for truth in religion. All I wanted was to stay drunk and high and await my execution. If I was going to be executed and go to hell anyway, I figured I might as well make some friends down there before I arrived.

When I was in the free world and used both alcohol and drugs, I was able to hold down a job. The job forced me to be active and always be on the move from place to place. This place had me caged in a cell where my movements were limited and therefore having a greater effect on me physically and mentally.

I became tired of the constant hangovers. The pills would sometimes cause my body to cramp up and render me unmovable for hours. The headaches were also constant. I was only 29 years old, yet I felt as if I was in my 60s. Officially, I wasn't under any kind of medication. All the drugs I was taking were from the black market. I was always on a constant search for someone looking to sell off their medications. My family continued to try and fill my mind with the things of Christ, and I continued to reject it. I was tired in every sense of the word: Emotionally, mentally, physically, and even spiritually. As much as I hated the name of Jesus Christ, I had been brought up in the church and in times of need we resort to what we know. Yes, I hated the name of Jesus Christ, but at the same time I knew that Christ was real and that there was power in His name. I'd been studying Satanism and black magic for a while. Even in the books I studied, they didn't deny that Christ was real and was the Son of God. They only denied His power and authority.

At first when I began to study the occult, I found it ironic and interesting that the Hebrew names of God are actually used to both threaten and tame demons. I also found it interesting that no other name was mentioned with that power, not Buddha, Krishna, Mohammed, or even Zeus. The only name that is above all other names in heaven and on Earth is the name of Jesus.

In a moment of desperation and despair, I found myself calling out to God wanting to change my life or at least wanting to change my circumstances. It wasn't a sincere cry for help. I really needed help but didn't want to change anything. As in the past, I was only crying out because of the situation I found myself in. I wanted God to help me in my situation, and I wanted Him to save me from depression and restore my health and strength. However, I didn't want God to change the way I was living, such as interfering with my drinking.

I've heard stories and I'm sure many have of people who have cried out to God and have felt an instant change. I felt absolutely no change physically, mentally, or spiritually. It was as if I'd cried out to the concrete walls surrounding me inside my prison cell. I decided to do a fast for a few days. I knew that there was power in fasting and prayer. Fasting is used in both Satanism and Christianity. In Satanism, fasting is done before certain rituals are performed, while in Christianity fasting is done as a way of humbling oneself to God. I began my fast on the first week of August. I hadn't set a number of days, but I wanted to just go as long as I could. It felt pretty good the first couple of days to give my body a break from all the constant punishments I was putting it through. By the fifth day I was still going strong as I'd taken no pills or alcohol, and although I was having a hard time sleeping, I was beginning to feel good physically.

While I wasn't feeling the power of God, I was feeling the results of my body releasing some of the toxins that I'd been feeding it daily for over a year and a half. The locker was still full of all kinds of occult books and materials. I had cried out to God, not wanting to let go of my obsessions and addictions, but God in His mercy touched me on Saturday, the fifth day of my fasting.

The section I was in had outside exercise areas, which we were allowed to use on Saturdays. The neat thing is that two inmates are allowed outside at the same time, but not within the same cage. The outside recreational yards are set up like this: There is basically one big box with 40 feet concrete walls surrounding it. It is divided down the center by prison bars and a metal mesh over the bars. Two inmates are allowed outside at the same time, but not on the same side, so that each one has his own yard. In addition to fresh air and exercise, it is a lot more quiet than the exercise areas on the inside. Outside, a person can have a one on one conversation without having to try to talk over several other people in the same section. I went outside that day with a friend who said that he was a Christian. I didn't mind going outside with anyone no matter what they believed in. He began talking to me about the Bible and that was okay, too, as I knew that most people didn't really know much about the book. I wasn't any kind of a Bible scholar, but I had grown up in the church and it was my clear impression that I had attained more knowledge than the other inmates. My friend came at me with some really off the wall ideology that I had never heard of and that really made no sense to me. It was funny that I was actually attempting to correct him when I myself wasn't a Christian, but I figured that since I was fasting and had called out to God, I could preach. We ended up spending the next four to five hours in the blazing summer heat due to some incident with the guards. When I finally got back to the cell I was completely exhausted. By this time, I had not eaten or drank anything in five long days. Inside, I felt defeated for some reason. I felt as if I'd lost some kind of battle that I was supposed to win because I was fasting. I asked myself why I had not been able to convince my friend that he was wrong in his beliefs. I was mad at God because I felt He had allowed me to look like a fool. I got on my knees and began to pray; however, rather than praying I was really just attacking God and accusing Him of not helping me explain His Word. I still held lots of anger and was attempting to take it out on God. My repentance had not been sincere from the beginning as I didn't want God – I only wanted His help. I was still holding on to everything of this world, including my selfishness and evil desires and thoughts.

After I was done praying and accusing God, I got off my knees. It was about 2:00 p.m., and I was feeling lightheaded, so took a short nap. That night I had what I truly believe was a vision from God. Some may say that I was only dehydrated and exhausted, and what I saw was only a result of that. However, I don't believe that because in the years to come, I would have other visions during times that I was neither tired nor dehydrated.

CHAPTER 12:
THE VISION

My vision began like this: I was seated in the back seat of a small car with my brother and sister. My father was behind the steering wheel, and my mother was next to him. We were driving through the middle of a city that was unfamiliar to me. As we drove down a trafficated street, my father suddenly hit the brakes and parked in front of a police station. It had a sign hanging from the entrance with a picture of what appeared to be a police badge. My father got out of the car and went into the building while we waited. Soon after, he came back – without saying anything. We continued on. It seemed to be a beautiful sunny day with the sun right behind us. We were headed toward a bridge that was in sight from the car. As we approached the bridge, it seemed as if it went on forever. It was a huge bridge not just in length, but in its totality, similar to the Golden State Bridge. It had the color of dark orange red. Massive steel cables were affixed to both sides to support it. It was a beautiful looking bridge that was suspended over a deep body of water. All around me were big fluffy clouds with a clear blue sky above me.

As we approached the bridge, I noticed the strong current of the ocean below us whose waves reached toward the clear blue sky. I was amazed at the power that the ocean demonstrated as its waves moved so fiercely and became agitated.

We entered the bridge alongside other cars. As I continued to stare at the waves, they continued to climb higher and higher and become stronger and stronger. Yet the day seemed as peaceful as could be.

We were somewhat deep into the bridge when all of a sudden it began to shake. At first, it was just a gentle trembling that could barely be felt, but I could see the suspension cables as they would gently become lax and then were pulled taut as the bridge settled back. The situation changed rather quickly as the trembling continued and became more violent. Before I knew it, the bridge was shaking violently and our car became airborne and then slammed back onto the pavement with a strong force.

I looked out the window and saw that the suspension cables began to snap like a burning piece of string. The road ahead was no longer straight but meandered into S-curves, and the ocean below us had become so fierce that the waves were turbulently crashing on the bridge and slamming onto the car. No one spoke a word, and I just continued to look at the chaos. With the suspension cables snapping off, the bridge no longer stood flat but hung at an angle. The pavement in front of us suddenly broke off leaving the car we were in with the front tires hanging off the bridge, while the back tires were still on the pavement. Through it all the sky remained clear and blue, giving no signs of the chaos that I was witnessing. Then it abruptly came to an end: The bridge stopped trembling, the waves stopped, and all seemed as if peace had suddenly been restored over everything. The bridge still remained damaged and leaning to one side.

I have never before experienced an actual earthquake, but if I had this is what I would imagine it would feel like. I am glad that I experienced it in a vision rather than in real life.

I got out of the car – I couldn't see any people. There were no other cars on the bridge, neither was my family there anymore.

Many of the suspension cables had snapped off and it seemed as if the bridge could fall completely at any moment. The sun continued to shine brightly, and the sky remained a beautiful shade of blue. The clouds made it seem as if it was a picture right out of a postcard. The more I looked around, the more I felt as if I was the last person on earth. The day seemed so picture perfect as if nothing had ever happened, except for the lopsided bridge. I began to walk back in the direction we had come from. I couldn't go the other way because the pavement had collapsed. As I walked down the long and lonely bridge, I took a peek over one of the edges at the ocean below me. The ocean seemed calm and pleasant as if inviting me to take a dip in its refreshing waters. I reached the entrance and continued to walk forward. I was again in the city we had passed during our drive. Everything still remained standing – the turbulence hadn't had any effect on the city, though there was still no one anywhere around. It almost felt eerie walking down the streets. I didn't know exactly where I was going, but I remembered that my father had walked into a police station, so I headed in that direction. I eventually reached that building and was suddenly stopped in the middle of the street by an extremely bright light that was directly in front of me. Out of reflex, I raised my hands to my face to shield my eyes from the brightness. The power of the light was massive and I could feel the light on me, as if the light rays themselves were embracing me. I slowly removed my hands from my face wanting to see what it was that was in front of me. The light dimmed a little, yet I could still feel its heat and embrace. A tall and dazzling being stood in front of me, blocking my way. The being had male features and was much taller than I was. He was dressed in a bright, white robe that emitted rays of light. It was as if it was made of light itself. I've seen beautiful artistic impressions of angels in paintings. Those paintings didn't compare to what I was seeing in front of me. I somehow knew that it was an angel standing there. It didn't only emit a bright embracing light, but also exuded a sense of peace and wonder and an authority that was beyond comparison. The angel stood there staring at me intensely but never uttering a word. I couldn't do anything but look at this majestic presence. It just stood there looking at me. I finally broke eye contact and looked around. I was still in the middle of the street in front of the police station. There were many buildings of different sizes and shapes. I expected the angel to say something to me, but it just stood there blocking my way and staring intensely at me. I instinctively knew that I wouldn't be able to go around the angel, so I didn't even try to. I didn't know what I was supposed to do next. Was I supposed to say something or do something? I was stuck there unable to go around it or to go through it.

Suddenly, out of the corner of my eye, I noticed something I had not seen before, or perhaps it was something that had just appeared. There was something in every window of every building I could see. It seemed as if there were many pairs of eyes staring at this confrontation between the angel and myself. I looked more carefully, and I was this time completely sure that there were many eyes observing us. Bizarrely, I couldn't see any pupils in the center of the eyes, and yet I was sure that they were all staring at me because I could feel their gaze. With the assurance of peace and safety radiating from the angel, I felt amazing. I had never felt such peace or safety. I looked toward the beautiful angel, and for the first time he spoke to me. I am not sure if he spoke to me audibly or if he used telepathy. What he said both surprised and intrigued me at the same time. The angel said, "They are surprised that you can see them, they are not used to people being able to see them." I suddenly realized that the eyes, I was seeing, belonged to demons. It was just unbelievable how many there actually were – yet they were confined to the buildings. Perhaps they were afraid of the angel. Those were the only words that the angel spoke to me – he never moved or faltered in his stance.

Just as fast as the trembling on the bridge had stopped, the demons and the angel disappeared. All now seemed normal as before the trembling of the bridge had taken place. The street had become busy again, like any other congested metropolis. I looked around me searching for the eyes that had been there at the windows just seconds ago, but they were all gone. I wondered what had happened to them. Were they still watching me, even though I couldn't see them? And what had happened to the angel that had been blocking my path, where had it gone to? Why had it stopped me in my tracks? It had said nothing to me other than to tell me that they were surprised that I was able to see them. Had he been sent to reveal something to me more by sight than by words? Could those demons actually hurt me, or were they just watchers? I no longer felt the peace and safety I'd felt when it had been standing in front of me, so if I was able to feel that then perhaps the demons could hurt me. There were just so many questions and no answers. I took a step forward and began to walk in no particular direction. I approached an intersection. When I had finally reached it, I turned to my right and continued to walk down the street observing my environs. As I walked, I came upon a house that looked as if it was out of place. I'd been walking in the business part of the city, but I had unexpectedly come across an old house that sat wedged in-between two commercial buildings. The house was remarkably run down and even spooky. In a way, it had probably been abandoned for some time. The house was wood-framed, rather rotten, and there were many gaping cracks that revealed the inner frame of the house. The paint was chapped and had lost its glow. The windows had been partially covered with pieces of plywood. As I was looking at the house, I somehow knew that a witch lived inside it. Strangely, I felt as if I needed to talk to the witch about something. Perhaps she could tell me why I had seen an angel and demons. I felt a strong pull toward the house as if someone was attracting me with a powerful human magnet. There was a small chest-high, chain-linked gate that I had to go through to get to the front door. Beyond the gate, there was a narrow bridge that led from the gate to the front door. I don't know what it was with bridges, but this was the second bridge I was seeing that day. Unlike the other bridge I had seen and very much felt earlier, this one was made of wooden planks attached to ropes that span across from the gate and ended at the front door. It also had a rope on each side to hold on to as a person made their way to the house. Below the bridge was nothing, other than absolute darkness. That darkness stood out as much as the house did. The small bridge was clearly unstable and unsecured, yet I knew that I had to get across it. I couldn't stop staring at the house. Could there actually be a witch inside? It just looked so abandoned, and what could she possibly have to tell me? I didn't know the answer to these questions, but the pull was too strong. I made up my mind to walk across the bridge. Before I could take a step toward the small gate, something in the sky caught my attention. It appeared to be a bright light that was descending from the sky towards me. Apparently it was a white dove approaching me. As it got closer, I stretched out my hand in front of me with the palm up, and it landed there. However, it wasn't a dove at all. It appeared to be a business card of some kind. Yet this was like no other that I had ever seen before. The card was shining so brightly that I was unable to read what it said. With the card in my hand, I no longer felt the need to go into the house. I no longer felt as if anything that witch had to tell me had any importance. I took a step back away from the gate. With the card still in my hand, I walked back passing the same storefronts and buildings I had passed minutes ago. I reached the intersection where I had made a right turn, but then I was stopped in my tracks by a big light that was blocking my path. The light was even brighter than the sun, and I could instantly feel its rays embrace me and I felt an overwhelming sense of peace and safety come over me. I reflexively raised my hands to shield my eyes, yet the light penetrated my hands. I felt the light as it dimmed down enough for me to be able to see that it was the same angel of God who had manifested itself earlier. I suspected that the eyes might have returned, but I couldn't see any in the buildings around me. I looked back toward the angel, and with his left hand he pointed to my right hand that was still holding the card. The card was completely blank except for one word that was written in the center of it, which said, ACCESSION. I read the word but it didn't have any significance to me, so I just dropped it to the ground. The angel quickly picked the card off the ground and handed it back to me and pointed at it. I read the word again. The card made no sense. Down to the ground it went again. With a swift movement, the angel grabbed it from the ground. He held the card in his hands and stared at me. He then spoke a single word to me in Spanish – which was *espera*, which in English translates to wait. He then handed the card back to me and pointed at it. I looked at the word, but I was lost as to its meaning and didn't really know how it related to me. The word, ACCESSION, was written in such beautiful script lettering, and the color was so bright that even solid gold could not shine as much. I was staring at the card when all of a sudden the card disappeared from my hands as did the angel. With that last view of the word, I woke up from my nap. The dream had felt so real, as if it had been something much more than just a dream. I kept wondering about the significance of the dream. Did it mean anything at all? It had been so detailed and felt so real. Who was the witch in the old house? Why had I seen an angel of God twice along with two very different bridges? What about the mysterious police station? More than anything, the thing that stood out the most was the word that had been written on the business card. I got off the bunk and did my normal routine. I brushed my teeth, washed my face, and got ready to face the rest of the day as it was still early.

Throughout the day, the word continued to pop in and out of my mind. I was not familiar with the word. I didn't even know its definition. The word was so strong in my mind that I ended up looking it up in a dictionary. What I found was that it has five different meanings. Two of those appeared to stand out with regard to my dream. The first was the act of coming or attaining a throne or power, and the second one was that it could mean to "increase by addition." As a Christian today, these two definitions have a strong meaning for me as they all came true when the Holy Spirit manifested himself for me. I believe that the dream foreshadowed my current life and it was something sent by God.

I felt pretty good that day after I'd woken up from my nap. I woke up feeling refreshed, knowing or at least believing that I'd seen a vision. However, the feelings of joy didn't last very long. That same evening I broke my fast when they served us dinner together with a piece of yellow cake with chocolate frosting. By the following week, I was back to my old ways of drinking and doing prescription medicine. My cry to God had not truly been sincere, and there had not been a true sense of repentance from me. My cry had only been empty words that had been blown with the wind the moment they had left my lips. I didn't really want to change my life. I only wanted my situation and surroundings to change. Satan had been working on me for a while, and his hands were tightly clutching my life. He wasn't going to let me go. Without the help of the Holy Spirit it was going to be impossible for me to change my life or even survive.

CHAPTER 13:
ENCOUNTER WITH SATAN

My depression, anger, and addiction continued to grow everyday as I fought my raging internal battle. There were days that my depression was so bad that I didn't want to get off the bunk or maybe it wasn't so much that I didn't want to get off the bunk, but rather I couldn't get off even if I had tried. I had given up my search for "truth." In my mind, I believed I'd found truth in Satanism and black magic. The truth I'd found was that there was freedom in Satan. It was only him who could give me freedom from the prison which was my own mind. It was also my conviction that he could help me get revenge on those who I held so much hatred for. I believed that Satan's power was equal to God's, and that God could be defeated. I couldn't see that I was being led down a path that would lead to self-destruction or annihilation. I couldn't see that what Satan was offering me was just more of what I'd had while I was free. My mind stayed in a constant fog because of all the pills I was popping. Yet even through that fog I continued to practice blood rituals and even began to increase them.

There are many branches of the occult, and each one has its own practices, rituals, and rites. Some are very different from each other, but lots of them use blood in their rituals whether human or animal. One practice I began was the art of astral projection and lucid dreaming. With time I mastered both of these satanic practices. It was through these practices that I learned to travel through the heavenly places that the Apostle Paul talks about in Ephesians 6:12 where it says, "For we do not wrestle against flesh and blood, but against principalities, against powers, against the rulers of darkness of this age, against spiritual host of wickedness in the heavenly places" (NKJV). In this verse, the Apostle Paul makes it clear that there is a heavenly realm where wickedness roams. This realm is apart from the realm in which we live in, yet has an influence on the things that happen here. Through astral projection and lucid dreaming, I learned to navigate through these realms. On many occasions, I made contact with the wickedness that was roaming in those realms.

Several months after I'd had my experience with the angel of God, I was moved to cell number 35, which was directly in front of the exercise yard. To me it didn't really matter what cell I was housed in as it was just another cell that was made of concrete walls and had a metal bunk. I continued with my satanic practices. I wanted to learn everything I possibly could about Satanism. I was determined to make contact with Satan himself and sign a pact with him face to face. From my studies, I knew that what I desired to do was almost impossible. Satan is not and cannot be omnipresent, and thus it is impossible for him to be in more than one place at a time. He desires to be like God who is omnipresent but will never reach his goal. Satan, for the most part, stays close to people of high influence and near places of power and people of political power. The majority of people who deal in the occult usually only deal with demons and fallen angels. Although, they may be high ranking fallen angels who hold extreme power, they are not Satan himself, but they will not hesitate to demonstrate that they, too, are powerful beings.

While in my new cell, I continued praying to Satan and performing blood rituals. This had become my normal activity before going to sleep. However, by the time nighttime would arrive, my mind was usually muddied from the drugs I'd used during the day; therefore, there were some nights where I just mumbled a prayer to Satan.

I had learned that in order to perform astral projection a certain measure of meditation was needed. This was sometimes a problem for me due to the effects of the drugs.

However, after much experimentation, I learned to somewhat control my high by choosing the right combination of pills. One night, I stepped out of my body in the form of a lucid dream. There have been times where I'd stepped out of the body and had found myself in the very cell I was sleeping in, except that I'd seen it through spiritual eyes. Yet, I'd known it had been the same cell. This time when I stepped out I didn't find myself in a cell, but rather found myself in a gym. This was really strange to me because I wasn't into fitness. Around me were several people dressed in workout clothes. It was as if they couldn't see me. I walked around in the gym and noticed that there were many doors along the walls. I picked one at random. Upon stepping through the door, I found that I was obviously no longer inside the gym. I now found myself in a long hotel hallway. There were doors on both sides and the hallway seemed endless. The place was full of people walking up and down. Many were coming and going, yet everyone was ignoring me. It was eerily quiet as I stood there just looking at everything that was going on. The hallway itself was dark though there was a lamp in-between each door. There was a dark, red colored carpet covering the floor with a red runner on top of it. The carpet was old and dirty. It even seemed as if there were small bugs crawling through the woven fabrics. The people that were in the hallway were well dressed, yet I noticed that their clothing was dirty and discolored. I took a step forward and began to walk down the hallway. I wondered what it was that was behind the doors. Did they all lead to the same place? Somehow, I knew my goal and that was to find Satan himself! I began to ask the people around me where I could find him. Some people would point me to a certain door, while some would point me toward another. Yet no one spoke a word to me, they would just look at me with a dead look and point me in a certain direction. The more people I asked, the more I noticed that they all had the same dead look. They looked like zombies. They seemed as if they were lost trying to find their own way home. I finally picked a door randomly and opened it. I couldn't see anything inside as it was pitch black. I stepped inside and found myself in another hallway. I stepped up to the door closest to me and turned the door knob and swung it open. I walked in and found myself in another hallway, if not the same. There were no longer any people walking around. I found myself alone in a dark endless hallway. I began running, although it seemed as if the scene didn't change. I wasn't getting anywhere. I tried entering other doors but ended up right back where I had started. I panicked. Suddenly, the doors were locked. I finally stopped and turned back. I had been running forward the whole time, perhaps I had to go the other way. However, what was behind me was identical to what was in front of me, nothing but a long dark hallway with doors on either side.

I finally managed to get through a door. To my surprise, I was in a huge room that exhibited both beauty and royalty. The dirty and stained red carpet and runner were nowhere to be seen. The room was huge but empty, except for torches that were affixed to the walls. They had huge flames that shot out of each lamp reaching several feet into the air. Yet, mysteriously, the room was dark. Every inch of the walls were covered in crown molding. The ceiling had a dome in the center, making it look even higher.

I hadn't yet moved, I couldn't move! All I could do was stand there amazed and in awe of the intricacy and grandiosity of the room. Due to the shadows that were playing off the torch lamps, it seemed as if the room was alive and moving. It seemed as if faces would come and go on the walls and the ground seemed to dance like the ocean. I was so caught up in everything that I was seeing that I initially had missed a massive staircase that was directly on the other side of the room. From where I stood, it seemed to blend into the marble flooring. There was nowhere else to go except toward the staircase. I cautiously took a step forward, and that's when it happened. I felt as if a weight had been dropped on my shoulders. It was a demonic presence that had fallen over my entire body. This was not the first time I had felt this presence, but it was the first time I had felt it so strong on me. A demonic or satanic presence has a very specific feeling to it. Such a presence attempts to reign and control people and kingdoms through fear and intimidation. As I continued to walk toward the staircase, the feeling of a demonic presence became stronger with every step I took. The floor seemed to be moving, and I felt as if I was actually walking on an ocean of sand while the faces on the walls seemed to pop out, taunting and mocking me every step of the way. As I got closer to the staircase, I noticed that they were much bigger than I'd first thought. The stairs were made of the same marble as the floor. The stairs, too, seemed to be moving as if they were escalators made of flowing sand. The stairs led high up and curved toward my right. The room in its entirety looked as if it belonged in a palace somewhere; perhaps, I was inside one of Satan's palaces.

I noticed a small child seated on the third step from the bottom. The demonic presence was extremely intense close to the staircase. The boy just sat there calmly looking at me. He seemed to be 10 or 11 years old and was well dressed in a gray two button suit with a white shirt underneath, but no tie. His hair was neatly parted on his left side and combed to his right. His skin was fair toned with blond hair. His eyes stood out to me more than anything else. I'd seen eyes like these before. They were solid white with no pupils in them. They shone bright on his face, and though he had no pupils in them I could feel his stare on me. Even though, he just a small boy he made me feel weak at the knees. There were two grown men standing there with the boy as if they were his bodyguards. They were both well dressed in suits and standing tall on either side of him. They too had fair toned skin and neatly combed blond hair. They were apparently identical to each other as if they were twins. Both were clean cut and resembled the secret service men who protect the president. They were both wearing black shades to cover their eyes even though the room was dimly lit. I didn't have to see their eyes to know that they were staring at me. I could feel their gaze on me down to my bones. It seemed that all eyes were on me.

I was very fearful of the child. How could he instill so much fear in me? Or was it really the men who were radiating with terror? I wondered if I could be hurt in a lucid dream like this one as the spiritual realm influenced the physical world. Though the air around me felt heavier and I was stuck in a state of awe and fear, I was finally able to gather my thoughts and set out to do what it was that I had come here to do. I asked the kid just one question, quite certain that the answer would be, "No," yet, I thought that maybe he could lead me in the right direction. I gathered my wits and asked him, "Are you the one I'm looking for?" He responded in a calm and beautiful sounding voice, "What is it that you want of me?" His lips never moved. I was shocked by his response. Had I heard correctly? Could he be the one I was searching for? I thought that was impossible. Yet I wondered to myself what it was that I was expecting. Was I really expecting for Satan to appear wearing red tights with horns coming out of his head and holding a pitchfork?

I asked him again, "Are you the one I'm looking for?" He responded again in same beautiful and calm voice, "I am. What is it that you want from me?" I could feel his every word crawling all over my body as if his words had become the very blood that flowed through my veins. I dropped to my knees with my head bowed low to the ground. I said, "I'd like to make a pact with you." He responded in the same manner he had the first time: "What is it that you want of me?" I slowly responded, "I'd like to make a pact with you, by asking three things of you in exchange for my soul and life and whatever else you want of me." Satan stared at me with menacing and penetrating eyes. He'd just sat there through this whole exchange not moving a single inch. The men who were behind him also just stood there unmoving and unflinching. He asked me again, "What is it that you want of me?" My heart felt as if it would beat right out of my chest. I could still feel the demonic presence over me like a weight and all around me like a cloud or fog that was unseen. I responded to Satan with my request, "My lord king and god, the first thing I ask of you is my freedom from prison." I looked up from where I knelt, but he seemed unmoving. He'd not reacted in any way. So I continued, "My lord king and god, I ask that I be given power to command demons in order to carry out your will." In addition to carrying out his will, I also wanted the power to carry out my own selfish and evil ambitions. I didn't get a reaction from him. He just sat there, and it gave me a bit of hope as he had not yet rejected my request. I went on with my last request, "My lord king and god, I ask that you grant me the power to torment each and every person that was in that courtroom with me during my trial in both this world and the next." It had taken me a long time to come up with these requests, but I knew this was what I wanted, and I was willing to do anything to get it, even if that meant spending eternity in hell. I remained on my knees before the child who had claimed to be Satan himself. I kept my head bowed to the ground waiting for him to respond by rebuking me, crushing me, or agreeing to this pact I'd presented before him. However, he remained silent for what seemed like an eternity. I didn't know how much more I could take as I felt like being crushed, and it seemed as if the longer I stayed there on my knees, the stronger the demonic presence became. He finally answered me and it was somewhat of a relief, the quietness had become extremely eerie and spooky. He spoke to me in a choir like voice, though it was flat and emotionless at the same time. He said, "I will give you two of the three things you've asked of me, but one of the things you've asked for is not mine to give." He wasn't being very specific. He then said to me, "Now I have a question for you." He then asked, "Are you ready to pass through the pain and sacrifice it will take for you to receive what you've asked of me?" His question caught me off guard. I wasn't expecting any questions and especially not one like this, but I didn't think twice about it. Still down on my knees with my head bowed to the ground I said, "YES!" Then he said to me, "Then you will pass through it indeed, and it will be done as I have said." With those final words ringing in my head I woke up.

I was covered in sweat and my heart was pounding inside my chest. I could still feel a lingering demonic presence in the air, as if it had carried over from the room I'd just been in. I got off the bunk and splashed some water on my face and thought to myself, "What a dream!" After doing my normal daily routine, I began my day. I had a lot of things that were running through my mind the whole day. Had I really made a pact with Satan himself? Could that really have been a meeting with Satan, or had that just been a really intense dream I'd had? It just somehow all seemed too easy to me, though he had said I would have to suffer in order to get what I'd asked for. I wondered what shape that suffering would come in, if it came at all.

The day was just another day on death row. I had somehow expected it to be different. After a long day of drinking and taking pills, I was finally ready to get some sleep. It seemed as if I needed an aid just to get some sleep so I swallowed a few

Benadryls along with some hooch. As usual before I went to sleep, I dropped down to my knees, performed a satanic ritual, and recited a satanic prayer. During my prayer, I asked Satan if the experience I'd had the night before was truly real. I asked him to demonstrate his power one more time to me by confirming what I had seen.

The thought that I'd actually met with Satan and made a pact with him was exciting and frightening at the same time. I went to bed and prepared my mind in meditation as I had learned to do. Every time I did it, it would take me less and less time to leave the body. It would sometimes take me several minutes to get my mind in a blank state which is required, but this time was very different. I got into a comfortable position and I closed my eyes and was instantly out of the body. This time there was no need for me to go through a bunch of doors searching for Satan. Satan was sitting in front of me no less than a few feet away from me. I was seated in the back seat of what appeared to be a limousine. All the windows were black, so I was unable to lookout and see where we were, or if we were moving at all. Satan sat in-between the two men who I had seen with him the night before. It is an unexplainable feeling to be that close to evil itself. It's a kind of mixture of fear and excitement intermingled with sadness and despair. Satan then asked me, "Why do you doubt me!?" Although the voice was the same as the night before, the feeling that it emitted was pure hatred. In his calm voice, he then said, "Do you not believe I could do what I have declared I will do?" His stare was penetrating down to my very soul and into my heart, making me shake. This was exactly what I had asked for before I'd entered the lucid dream. I worked up the nerve to respond. I said, "Forgive my doubtfulness, but remember that I am merely dust, and the seed of doubt has been planted in my heart since my birth." I didn't know what else to say. I had doubted not only him but the whole experience.

With that same hatred that could be felt in his every word, but not heard, he said, "Never doubt me! If I have said I will do something then I will do it!" And with those final words I was roused awake with my heart pounding out of my chest and covered in sweat. I was waking up more and more at all hours of the night with my heart pounding and drenched in sweat. I had gotten my confirmation from Satan himself. The whole experience had seemed so swift since so little had been said, but it had actually taken the entire night.

I truly believed that Satan was all powerful and that he was in control, not only over my life, but even my death. I understood that he was a created being, yet I also believed that since he was God's first created being, he'd been given powers that no other being had. After all, I'd read that one third of the angels in heaven had left it with him. I rationalized that if they no longer wanted to be in the so-called paradise, then there had to be something wrong with it, and if Satan and his angels didn't want anything to do with it, then neither did I. I felt as if I had a deal with death itself and a partnership with Satan.

CHAPTER 14:
GASSED AND SENT TO THE F-POD

After this experience I continued to live my life as I had been doing so for a few years. I still found it hard to believe that I had accomplished what I desired. Even though I still found myself in prison, I knew I had a powerful advocate behind me, despite knowing that this pact was of no help to me in the natural world. Without realizing it, my addictions and depression continued to tighten their grips on me. I guess that in my ignorance I still hadn't grasped the danger that came with practicing the occult. Had I been more wise I would have realized that Satan has an ultimate plan for not only my life, but for all those who choose to rebel against Jehovah God.

I was reading everything I could get my hands on that talked about satanic and black magic practices. Cutting myself had become a norm and an easy thing to do. On some occasions, I would attempt to buy blood from other inmates who were around me. I'd offer to buy them a few dollars' commissary for some drops of blood. Some would look at me as if I'd lost my mind, while others really gave it some serious thought as they had no income. Some of the Christians on the pod completely avoided me. I guess they saw me as a waste of time, or too far away from their reach. However, I didn't care what they thought of me. I knew that one day my god would defeat theirs, and I knew that I had power that they could only dream of. After all I'd actually seen my god, which was much more than I was sure they could say.

I got much better at lucid dreaming and astral projection as I was practicing it every night. I loved navigating the heavenly realms and seeing new places. I saw it as my temporary escape from the prison walls. I still wasn't sure how badly I could get hurt in the physical world if I was killed or somehow else negatively affected in the spiritual one. It wasn't something that I really wanted to find out. I continued to travel to different places and meet many demons along the way.

Every time, I woke up from a lucid dream, a demonic presence lingered in the room. This was just another constant reminder of the blood pact and that gave me a sense of strange comfort. I was tightly in Satan's grip and I didn't want him to let me go. I had convinced myself that Satan was god, and that I'd found truth and the power I'd been looking for. The pain and suffering that Satan had told me I would have to go through had not yet come. I always kept those words at the forefront of my mind, always expecting them to come to pass. My mom and dad and the rest of my family continued to visit me. Every time they visited was like an act in a play I had to perform. I continued attempting to hide the life I was living in prison from them. Just like in the county jail, they would pray at both the beginning and end of every visit. I hated it as they would be praying to God to protect me! I found myself praying at the same time to Satan that he would not allow all the demons I'd invoked to be cast out of me.

Back then, I never reflected upon the fact that both my mom and dad had the power to cast out my demons. All I knew was that I didn't want it to happen. They had cost me too much time and blood to invoke, just to have them cast out so easily. My parents knew that something was wrong with me, no matter how good I faked a smile. There were only two people in my family who knew that I'd begun to dabble in the occult. One of them once asked me if I truly believed I'd found "truth" in Satan. I said, "Yes." She then asked why I didn't share that truth with my nieces who were like daughters to me. That was a powerful question. I really had no answer that made any sense. I knew that what I'd found was truth, although it was true evil. I was full of anger and full of rage. I knew the difference between good and evil. I had just chosen evil and I didn't want that for my nieces. I was only thinking of myself and the revenge I wanted to get against the people who had judged me.

My family continued praying for me together with their large Christian community. This was a mission in futility because the satanic seeds in me were deeply rooted. For some reason, Satan directed my anger toward my brother who had always been there for me since my childhood. My brother and I have always had a really strong bond. Yet for no reason whatsoever I had grown angry with him. Satan and his demons were filling my mind with all kinds of evil thoughts. Many times it was my brother who took the brunt of it all with the words and insults I threw his way. Today, I feel the pain and shame of the things I said to him, but I thank God that both God and my brother have forgiven me.

I would spend many days and nights in my cell drinking and plotting all the evil I wanted to inflict upon numerous people. My heart raged with anger and my bones shook from the frustrations of not being able to carry out the deeds I had envisioned. It is a horrible thing to be enslaved by the invisible enemies of this world. I found myself ensnared by depression, oppression, rage, and rancor, not to mention the enemies I could see, like alcohol. How can we fight what we cannot see? How can we fight against an enemy who doesn't bleed as we do? The answer is that it is impossible – at least not on our own.

One of my friends, Rolo, was in the recreational area that was directly opposite my cell, and we were able to comfortably talk with each other. Rolo was not as heavy a drinker as I was. There were only a few people in here who could have reasonably challenged me in a drinking contest. Another friend of ours had brewed and sent us both four bottles of hooch. Four bottles were usually enough to make a person pass out. For me, that was just enough to get me started. By the time Rolo started on his fourth bottle, he was already drunk, while I had begun to drink some of the hooch I had in storage. After he had finished his hooch, I sent him a couple more, although he really didn't need any extra. When his recreational time was over and it was time for him to go back to his cell, he was so drunk that he had to hold himself up from falling. He had already vomited twice.

When the guards came to escort him back to the cell, he was asked to take off his clothes as is the norm. I moved away from the cell door to give him some privacy as we all do (apart from a few exceptions) when someone is stripping naked. As he was undressing, I heard one of the guards laugh and I assumed that he was mocking Rolo. I figured he fell or something due to being so drunk. I later found out that the guard had not been scornful toward my friend. Instead, he had been talking to another inmate whose cell was also in front of the exercise area. Not knowing that at the moment and being drunk myself, I took offense at someone laughing at Rolo, especially when he was too drunk to defend himself. I took it personally and began to cuss the guard out, since I felt it was my fault for getting Rolo so drunk and putting him in that situation. We had a heated exchange that got me enraged. I was loaded up on pills and hooch and was ready to release some of that built up tension that had been accumulating for months.

Rolo was taken back to the cell and I continued to drink while shaking with rage. I couldn't stand the thought that someone had laughed at a friend of mine. I decided, the next time the guards passed in front of my cell, I was going to splash a liquid on them. I didn't know exactly what I was going to use, but I knew I wasn't going to use hot water or anything foul, like feces like many people do back here. I knew that by doing this, I was basically sending myself to the F-pod, which is the disciplinary pod, but I wasn't thinking straight at that moment as anger and drunkenness had taken a toll on my cognitive faculties. Then I got an idea: I filled up a shampoo bottle with water from the sink. The next time they passed by the front of the cell, I splashed the water on them. The guard who got hit by the water screamed. They ran out of the section while cussing at me. About ten minutes later, two sergeants came to the door holding a shield that covered the cell door. I continued to drink casually in the cell while the sergeants attempted to talk me out of the cell without having to call a "suit up team." I knew I was headed to the F-pod, so I figured I might as well drink the rest of my hooch and make them work for it. The sergeants finally got tired of dealing with me and called a suit up team. One of the sergeants left to suit up himself and gather the rest of the team. The suit up team is technically called an "extraction team." It usually consists of six of the biggest men they have on staff. They get geared up in full riot gear, including gas masks, helmets, knee pads, and elbow pads. The first one on the team carries a large riot gear shield. It took the team about 15 minutes to get ready and geared up. During that time, I continued to drink attempting to finish all the hooch I had left. When they arrived in front of the cell, I had about six bottles left. I'd already drunk seven or eight bottles. By this time I was extremely intoxicated, so much that I was leaning against the wall to hold myself up. I continued to drink because I knew I was about to spend at least 90 days on the F-pod, and it would be hard for me to find any hooch during those days. As the team stood in front of the cell, they attempted to intimidate me as is their protocol. It might have worked had I not been so drunk. One of the sergeants who were there gave me a direct order to strip off and submit to be cuffed. I refused by cussing him out and taking another swig of hooch. I had really upset the sergeants as I was making them work. One of them shot me with a blast of pepper spray from a can that had the size of a fire extinguisher. The shot hit me directly in the face as I had only been standing about three feet away from the cell door. The gas instantly blinded me. However, when you've lived in a cell for so long you instinctively have an orientation of everything around you.

I fumbled with my eyes closed, grabbed another bottle, and chugged it down. Then I reached for the next one and the next one after that. I knew that I had about a three minutes interval before I got sprayed again. I began to gag and choke as the gas did what it is designed to do. With my adrenaline pumping I continued to chug bottle after bottle despite the effects of the gas. The sergeant ordered me to strip naked and to submit to handcuffs. I responded by cussing him out. He then sprayed me a second time. My skin was on fire and I was completely blinded. The second time the tear gas was sprayed I made a mistake of breathing through the mouth instead of shallow breaths through the nose. The gas travelled straight into my lungs and shut down my respiratory system. I knew I had one more time before the team came in to forcefully extract me from the cell. Even so, I had already done what I wanted to do, which was to drink all the hooch, so there was no more point in refusing. I complied with their demands, and I was on my way to the F-pod for the first time.

CHAPTER 15:
AMARRE

When I arrived at the F-pod, my skin was on fire and I was still blind from the gas. The sergeants, who had escorted me, knew that this was not my normal behavior, so therefore I assume that this was the reason why they didn't want to inflict more suffering on my part, which they have done to others in similar situations. The sergeants asked me if I wanted a shower before I went into the cell. I obviously said, "Yes." Unfortunately, this was a horrible mistake! For some reason or another, water intensifies the burning sensation caused by the gas. Still handcuffed, I was put in the shower for about 30 seconds and then escorted into a cell. The minute I got into the cell and the hand restraints were taken off, I passed out on the hard metal bunk. I fell asleep with the gas still on my skin as the shower had not removed any of it. I was so drunk that I no longer felt the burning sensation – all I could feel was the cell spinning. This was going to be a bad hangover!

I woke up the next morning with someone calling my name from the recreational area, "Cortez! Cortez! Wake up you drunk!" I finally woke up with a killer hangover. I frantically looked around me, not sure where I was, and saw an empty cell. My mouth was dry and I had a throbbing headache. My skin was on fire from head to toe, and all I was wearing was a pair of boxer shorts. I couldn't remember everything that had happened the night before. I just smiled to myself. It was about 7 a.m. when my friend, Frankie, had woken me up. I got up and noticed that he was in the recreational area. He had come to the F-pod a few months back when he had been caught cooking hooch, which I found ironic. Frankie took one look at me and laughed like never before. My face was completely red from the gas. He said, I looked like the devil, all covered in red like that. I didn't have a mirror so I had no idea of the horrors that the mirror would have conveyed to me. He asked me what had happened and I told him what I could remember. He laughed through the whole story, and at the end, I had to laugh too. It was just another page in the story of my life. I tried to wash off the gas, but the water just made it worse. What I needed was some really heavy duty soap. After Frankie went back to his cell, another friend of mine was taken to the exercise area. After I had told him the story, he gathered a few items for me that I would need, like soap, toothpaste, and a toothbrush. The best part was the bag of coffee he had also given me. He also told me how to remove the gas by using cold water. He said that hot water opens up your pores and lets the gas in, which is why it burns more. He had been to the F-pod many times through his years on the row. Things worked differently on F-pod than they did elsewhere in the prison. For the most part, the guards left people alone there as they knew that you were already there for causing trouble. So there wasn't much more they could do to you.

I was kept in the cell, without my property, for 72 hours as is the policy. After the time had passed, I was given my "level 3 property." There are three different levels that are used to classify death row inmates. Level 3 is considered the punishment level, and it is the lowest level that a death row inmate can be classified. While you have that classification, you are usually housed on the F-pod. All of your electronics are removed from your normal cell and stored with your other belongings in the property room. While on the F-pod, you are allowed to purchase writing materials and selected hygiene items. Worse yet is that you are limited to $20 in correspondence materials, stamps included. Your time in the exercise yard is also reduced. There are many other restrictions as well. The worst one is that you are only allowed one visit a month while you are a level 3 prisoner. When you eventually become reclassified to a level 2 prisoner, which lasts for at least 60 days, you can receive two visits per month, and you will get your reading materials. If you don't receive an infraction for those 90 days, you will be able to leave the F-pod and get your electronics back. During my time there, I had a hard time focusing on writing and reading, and I couldn't get my hands on hooch. I did, however, get plenty of psychiatric medication. They seemed to be handling it out like candy. I wasted away the days lying on the bunk sleeping. With the absence of alcohol, the sense of gloom, despondency, and weary hopelessness entered my mind like never before.

The cell I had been confined to seemed perfect for what I had dedicated my life to. Whoever had been in it before me had done a number on it. The metal bunk had a satanic prayer engraved into it. The prayer covered the whole bunk. There were also satanic prayers written on every inch of the concrete walls. The concrete floor had a pentagram drawn at the center. I was feeling extremely lonely during those days as a level 3 prisoner. I was fortunate to have friends, on the other side of the pod, who were able to get me plenty of coffee and other foods from the canteen. However, regardless of material goods, my heart was troubled and I urgently needed help.

As I became a level 2 classified death row inmate, I was dying of boredom and eventually decided to dedicate the next 60 days to satanic rituals and a deeper study of the occult. I wasn't interested in recruiting fellow inmates into these practices. I considered it a private matter between me and Satan. However, I did become friends with my neighbor who showed some interest in what I was practicing, although he was a bit skeptical. I understood his fears and how unnerving it can be to meet someone who professes Satan's sovereignty. One thing led to another, and I began to teach him simple satanic prayers. I also shared all of my knowledge regarding the occult with him, yet he continued to be doubtful. I decided to show him that this was real. I showed him how to do an "amarre," which in Spanish translates to "a bonding or a tying." This was one of the easiest rituals I had learned to do. Everything that we receive in prison has to pass through the hands of the unit's mailroom. It is usually them who decide if we are allowed to have an item or not. There are some things that are scrutinized more than others. For example, we are not allowed any books that describe rape scenes or magazines that may have sexually explicit images. I ended up doing an amarre toward the mail room in order to blind them to the packages I was receiving. I wasn't ordering anything that was illegal, just a bunch of pornographic materials that I knew would be denied, especially since I was a level 2 prisoner. When my mail would arrive with every single piece of material I'd ordered, my friend would have nothing to say. My neighbor then began to believe that my satanic rituals were working miracles. The whole time I was in that cell I was never denied anything that I really wanted to get that came through the mailroom.

I had finally gone through all my reading materials at least twice as I had no radio and nothing else to do all day. I ended up ordering several more books from a company I had been buying my occult books from. Most of the books I had ordered were not of any use to me. They had interesting titles, but were all written for mass production and didn't really get deeply into what I was looking for. However, one of the books I ordered was solely based on black magic rituals and its history. This one book alone piqued my interest. It was very well written and very detailed. It spoke of rituals performed a long time ago on actual animal skins and about various animal sacrifices. It broke down the names of many demons and what some of their powers were. I was shocked that I'd met some of them in my dreams. One of the chapters that hit me the hardest was one that spoke of the appearances of Satan himself. As I was reading it, there was a part that explained that when Satan appears to people he usually does it in the form of a "comely child." It also said that Satan always has two acolytes with him. When had I read this, I felt a chill running down my spine and I got goose bumps all over my body. I couldn't believe what I'd just read! I was at this time completely sure that the pact I'd made with the child, a couple of months before, had been real and binding. It had been Satan himself. It was frightful to read in a book that I'd never read what I'd experienced. This brought me a momentary smile. After 90 days in "the hole," I was moved back to the other level 1 prisoners.

CHAPTER 16:
DEMONS

I arrived at the C-pod on a mission to find hooch. There was always someone either willing to give me some bottles or sell me a few. I had not been drunk for a long time and was ready to wet my beak and quench my thirst. A friend of mine sent me a few bottles. Since my tolerance level had decreased in the last couple of months, I felt the old sensation of alcohol burning its way down my throat and into my belly. For some reason, I stopped practicing my rituals and satanic prayers. My depression was bad and my health was deteriorating completely. I weighed around 255-265 pounds. I was slowly killing myself with the weight of oppression that was on me, not to mention high blood-pressure and high cholesterol and the effects they were having on me.

I wasted away many more months in my cell. It seemed as if all I'd been doing was wasting away, just waiting to be executed. Being restricted in our movements the way we are, it was easy to fall into a daily routine. The days began to run together and one can easily begin to lose track of time. I have known many men behind these bars who never use a calendar because here there is no difference between Monday and Friday. It was getting harder and harder for me to find a reason to get off the bunk every day. There was nothing I looked forward to anymore. Yes, I enjoyed the visits from my family; however, even those took a toll on me emotionally and I also had to restrain my drinking and fake a smile.

Several months later, I was moved. Behind these prison bars we have no say in cell allocation. I was moved to the A-pod this time. This would be my first time. I already knew this was the pod where the men who have execution dates were housed. This is a place of horror – if not because of having received an execution date then because of having to watch close friends walk to their deaths. I understand that there are some who believe this is exactly what we deserve. I wouldn't fault anyone for feeling that way. I see it as a human reaction toward someone whom they feel has hurt them. I felt the same way for many years before Christ changed my life.

The men who have their execution dates scheduled are housed in the A-section. I was housed in the C-section. A-pod has a very different feeling from all the other pods. As soon as you walk into it, you can feel the oppression coming out of it. This makes the air heavy and difficult to breath. As a believer, I have come to recognize it as a demonic presence that hovers throughout the whole area. I've been told several horror stories by guards who have seen shadows moving inside of cells that they know to be empty. This is not so hard to imagine when one remembers that this is the house of death.

While housed there, I met another inmate who I had heard was also a Satanist. He was housed just a couple of cells from me. When we first met, we talked for a while and I shared some of the experiences that I'd been through since I began practicing the occult. He was taken aback by the rituals. He told me that he didn't like the sight of blood, especially his own. I understood exactly how he felt. I'd felt the same way for a long time until I got used to seeing and drawing my own blood. Our conversation was really of no benefit to me as I felt he practiced a watered down version of Satanism. However, the conversation awakened in me the desire to begin practicing my rituals. It didn't take me long before I was again traveling through the heavenly realms and slicing myself to carry out my rituals. Later, I got the news that when I had been gassed in cell number 35, the cell door had somehow been broken. It had been left empty until the door was finally fixed several weeks later. When it was fixed, a young man who had only been on the row for about three years was put there. Two weeks after housing him in that cell, he committed suicide. Upon hearing it, I instantly remembered all the rituals I had performed inside it. That had been the cell were I had made my pact with Satan. I began to wonder if perhaps he had been tormented by the demons I had evoked while in that cell. I'd learned that there are some demons that are very territorial and only stay in certain areas. I wondered if one of those demons had maybe driven him into madness and ultimately suicide.

I had several more experiences dealing with demonic forces while housed on the A-pod. One of the experiences was through a lucid dream. I had an out of body experience and found myself in a big bedroom. The furniture was antique yet clean and in a new condition. There was a big, oak colored four post bed in the center of the room. The bedding was soft, very expensive, and inviting. There was also a chandelier hanging low from the center of the ceiling which lit the room in a yellowish light. I was sitting on the floor with my back to the side of the bed and my legs stretched out in front of me. Sitting in between my legs was a beautiful woman who had her back against my chest. I was caressing her and had not noticed that there was another woman sitting on the bed. She sat on the side of the bed with the back of my head in-between her legs.

As I was caressing the woman on the floor, the second lady was massaging my neck. The woman sitting on the bed then reached down and grabbed my right hand and brought it up to her mouth as if to give it a gentle kiss. When she raised it to her mouth, I watched as she opened her mouth wide and bit into my hand. Right before she bit me, I was able to see that she had a mouth full of fangs. I let out a loud scream and tried to jerk my hand back, but she had a tight grip on it. She continued to bite down on my hand and I could feel intense pain shooting through my whole body. I guess this answered my question on whether I could be hurt during a lucid dream or not. I felt the woman who was on the floor with me begin to stir, and as I turned toward her, she began to attack me as well. The one who was still biding my hand was no longer the beautiful woman I'd seen earlier. She had become a horribly looking demon with fangs as teeth.

I attempted to fend them off as the woman on the ground attempted to reach for my throat. She, too, was no longer beautiful, but a dreadfully looking demon with two rows of fangs in her mouth. I began to fight for my life. I was able to pull my hand free, and I shoved my shoulder into the other one as I jumped up to my feet. As I got to my feet I got into a fighting stance ready to defend myself from the next attack that I was sure was coming, but it never came. They were both gone. They had vanished into thin air. I looked around and saw that on one of the walls, there was a demon menacingly watching me and laughing; it was a beast with some human features like hands, eyes, and legs. Its laughter, which was thunderous, hideous, and evil, seemed to shake the room. I quickly pulled myself together and woke up. As always, I woke up sweating profusely with my heart throbbing as if ready to jump out my chest. After I regained some calm and composure, I began to laugh at both myself and at the whole situation. Importantly, I had learned that it was possible for me to feel pain while traveling through these realms, and I'd also learned that it was possible for me to defend myself from attacks even those from the underworld. I had another encounter that for the first time jolted me into the realization of how dangerous what I was doing was. By this time, I had gotten really good at leaving the body through lucid dreaming. I was practicing it every night as I saw it as an escape from the reality of the prison cell. It was in the same way that I found an escape in alcohol and drugs, except this was somehow more real to me. On this particular night, after doing my usual prayers and rituals, I went to bed and soon after I was out of the body. I was in the middle of some kind of grand celebration, standing in the middle of a grand banquet hall with all the trimmings. I was surrounded by tables with beautiful laced table cloths laid over them. Each table was covered with delicious food platters. Even the chairs that were around the tables were decorated with expensive cloths edged with lace. There were also lots of people all around me coming and going in-between the tables. Most were carrying plates piled high with food.

I began to walk around and just take in the room and the people. Then it hit me! These weren't people at all: they were demons! At first they appeared human. However, upon closer inspection I saw that they had grotesque features. They all had eyes without pupils and their skin was tightly stretched around their animal-like features. Realizing where I was, I went on my knees and began to recite a satanic prayer. After repeating this prayer a second and a third time, I opened my eyes and saw that the demons had disappeared. Surprisingly, I found myself in the grand banquet hall all by myself. Nothing else in the room had changed. The tables still held all the platters piled high with delicious foods (every prisoner's day dream!). Suddenly a demonic presence hit me like a fist, and I looked around seeking the source, and then I saw him! There was a lone figure sitting on a chair in the corner of the room. He was unmoving. He just sat there looking at me with his pupil-less eyes. He had a snout like a pig and was partially covered in black hair. The places that didn't have hair, like his hands and face, were as black as coal. I could feel his gaze on me from across the room. I began to walk toward him, and the closer I got the stronger I felt his presence.

I was no longer seeking Satan as I felt our pact was a done deal. I only sought to meet other powerful demons who I believed I could make an alliance with. There was something different with this encounter. There was something I'd never encountered happening right before my eyes. I was shaken and confused. Why was this demon alone? In all my travels, I'd never encountered a lone demon. There had always been three or at least two that could be seen, and a third would show up at some point. I was cautious of the fact that not too long ago I'd been attacked. I wanted to make sure that there were none who could creep up on me from behind. I saw nothing. The room was eerily quiet, and everything around me appeared to be undisturbed. He never removed his gaze from me as I got closer to him. I got close enough to the point where I could reach out and touch him, though I dared not even attempt it. My plan was to bend the knee before him and see who he was and what rank he held. Before I could even bend the knee, he reached out in a flash and took my right hand with his left hand in a vise grip tight hold. As he held my hand, he still had not spoken a word. He just stared into my eyes. I unsuccessfully tried to pull my hand away from. He squeezed my hand tighter as I tried to jerk it away from him. I used every ounce of strength I had in me to try to break free. I couldn't. His arm was like a stiff metal rod. I panicked. I'd felt many other emotions and actual feelings in my previous out of body experiences – however, not once had I felt this way. Now my breath had been knocked out of my lungs somehow, and I felt immense pain everywhere. I couldn't even scream for help. I dropped to my knees as my legs could no longer sustain my weight. When I'd first begun practicing astral projection and lucid dreaming, one of the first things I'd learned to do was how to return to the body. I already knew I'd be seeing things that I might not really want to see, and I wanted a way to return to the body quickly. As I dropped to my knees, I began to shake my head from side to side as if saying, "NO!" This had been my strategy to come back into the real world. It did not work this time. Something had gone wrong and I couldn't wake up! The pain was pulsing throughout my whole body, as I continued to shake my head from left to right. I could feel my lungs collapsing from a lack of oxygen. I looked up and saw the demon staring at me with those penetrating evil eyes. He somehow knew exactly what I was trying to do by shaking my head, and he let out a reverberating mocking laugh. The demon continued to squeeze my hand so tight that it felt like my bones would begin breaking any second. I thought it was all over for me. My vision began to blur due to being overwhelmed by pain. He continued to laugh at my attempts to return to my body. I felt my lungs were about to implode, and I was only moments from passing out. I gave in to whatever it was that was going to happen next. If this was to be the end then so be it. There was nothing I could do. However, just before I passed out, the demon let go of my hand and I immediately woke up.

I woke up grasping at my chest and taking in deep breaths as if my head had been held underwater for too long. I had never been unable to return and wake up at will, and the presence that I was feeling in the cell was not a lingering presence. I felt as if the demon was in the cell with me staring at me. Even if I could not see him I knew he was there. The whole encounter had been different from the very beginning. From the first time I noticed that the demon was alone, I should have known something was off, but I just couldn't accept or wouldn't accept that these demons actually wanted to hurt me. I was on their side! I'd made a pact with Satan, and I felt that the pact superseded any authority these demons might have had on me. In any event, there were definitely some demons that were not honoring my pact.

CHAPTER 17:
WAITING FOR SATAN

I'd been on Texas death row for about four years, and I loathed every minute spent there. My only escape was drinking and doing prescription drugs as I listened to the radio and imagined myself on the outside. My lifestyle was beginning to take a toll on me in every way: physically, mentally, and spiritually. I always felt heavy and tired and it wasn't just due to the 265 pounds I weighed. Despite the fact that demons are spiritual beings, they were weighing down on my soul. I'd opened myself and willingly invited many of them to the point where I couldn't even begin to guess how many I had inside of me, not to mention those that crept in unbeknownst to me.

Most days, I felt as if my body and soul were just dragging on the floor. Many times I could feel the demons in me at war with each other for dominion over me. They weren't fighting against me as I had no energy to put up a resistance. The feeling is hard to explain as they attack your mind, spirit, and physical self all at the same time as each one has control over a certain part. However, I continued to be faithful in my prayers and rituals, always seeking to further my life through occult practices. Some of the rituals and bindings I'd performed had worked as the one I'd done toward the mailroom, but this was nowhere near the power I was looking for. I continued to read and study everything I could get my hands on that had to do with the occult. I also continued to travel through the spiritual realms. This had become the norm for me every night. I wasn't always seeking out Satan or demons in my travels. There were times I'd just visit other places and enjoy the views and surroundings. On other occasions, I'd step out of the body directly into a demonic realm. On one of these occasions, I found myself sitting in a small squared one-person sofa made of very soft cushions. In front of me and on either side were matching sofas with a demon sitting in each of them. The room was dimly lit. They were looking in my direction. They had human shaped bodies. However, they had heads like birds. Their bodies were draped in expensive looking business suits, but no matter how nice their clothing was, their heads were terrifying and horrifying to look at. These weren't your everyday hummingbird heads: The demons had the heads of birds that resembled something out of the Jurassic era. They all had long beaks that were clearly sharp to the touch. Their eyes were also elongated and were solid black, while their bodies from the neck down appeared to be human-like.

They sat there for what felt like a few minutes with none of them saying a word to me. Perhaps they were letting me take the situation in. The demon who was sitting in front of me finally began to speak. Apparently, he used telepathy as his beak never moved. The two that were on either side of me never said a word or moved a single muscle. We began discussing my case of all things. The demon began to ask me about my appointed lawyers and whether they were doing a good job or not. If I had been smarter, I would have realized that if they didn't even know what was going on in my case, they wouldn't have been able to sway the outcome in any way.

Interestingly, I noticed that for the first time in all my encounters I'd had in the past, these demons were not attempting to intimidate me or cause me fear of any kind. Though there heads were hard to look at without cringing, I felt no kind of aggression coming from them. The mood was rather calm and comfortable, like having a conversation with old friends. We continued our conversation and discussed some of the issues that were being raised on my appeals in detail. Toward the end of our conversation, the demon asked me if I was satisfied with the work my lawyers were doing. I thought about the question for a moment before I answered. I believed that they, along with Satan, had the power to do all things, including reaching the outcome I desired. So I told him that as long as they were controlling the situation I was satisfied. I never saw these demons again or any that looked like them.

CHAPTER 18:
"NO I WORSHIP SATAN!"

One of my last experiences with lucid dreaming has affected me in a major way to this date. It wasn't until years later that I understood the significance of the things I saw and felt. Due to this vision, as a believer in Jesus Christ today, I have felt the need to share the gospel of Jesus Christ, not only with those who will give me a few minutes of their time, but also with the world. I still do not know why God chose me of all people to see the things I saw. I know that I am the least deserving of all His servants, but I am grateful that He did. In my vision, I found myself lying on a bunk inside a small room, exactly as I found myself in the real world. I was asleep when I was suddenly awakened from my peaceful slumber by a powerful, bright light. I quickly sat up on the bunk and saw that there were two big and bright angels in the room. The angels were standing against a wall toward the foot of the bunk. The room measured about 10 feet in height and their heads reached the ceiling. I took a moment to look at them and take in their beauty. They were dressed in long bright white robes. On their waists were belts that shone bright as if made of solid gold. They both had a beautiful set of wings on their backs that shone as bright as their robes.

I sat there in awe of the beauty and size of these angels. Their eyes were beautiful and held me captivated. Unlike the demons I'd seen in the past, these eyes I was looking at seemed sympathetic toward me, and they had pupils in them. The angel that was standing closer to my right took a step forward and approached the foot of the bunk. I could feel that he held power and demanded respect. I sat there paralyzed and mute – lost in his power and beauty. The angel spoke words to me that, in the real world, I didn't want to hear. His words were soft spoken, full of love and compassion. He sounded truly sincere when he said, "It's not too late, come to Him, He will forgive you." I didn't understand what he was talking about at first. It wasn't too late for what? Who did they want me to come to? And what exactly did I need forgiveness for? None of this made any sense to me; however, one thing was certain and undeniable, and that was that these angels gave me a sense that was the opposite of every encounter I'd ever had with a demon. After a few moments, I realized or rather understood what the angel meant by what he had said to me, but with my mind and heart being as rebellious as they were, I wanted nothing to do with what he was offering. I responded to the angel with the first thing that came to my mind by saying, "NO! I worship Sata…." My lips became instantly sealed before I was able to finish saying my statement that I worshipped Satan. I'd been somehow stopped midway through the name of Satan. I tried speaking or screaming – but it was no use! My lips had been sealed shut. Again the angel spoke to me in the soft spoken voice, and said, "It's not too late, come to Him, He will forgive you." My mind was filled with evil and my heart had been turned to stone a long time ago. I was unable to finish my sentence. I was furious on the inside! How could he just shut my lips this way? I sat there on the bunk staring at this angel with furious anger and rage in my eyes. The angel continued looking at me with love and compassion in his eyes. All I could do was sit there and stare at him as I was no match for him or his power. The second angel who had remained against the wall had just stood there observing the whole time. He took a step forward and approached the bunk. He then spoke to me in a voice that was just as soft and sweet to my ears as the other angel's, but his words were different. He looked directly into my eyes and said, "Don't call on his name because he will come." I knew exactly who he was talking about. I knew exactly who it was they did not want me to call. That was exactly who I wanted to call upon. Yet my lips were still sealed and I was unable to call upon anyone. When the angel had said these words to me, he had not said them with any fear in his voice. Instead, it had sounded as a kind of loving warning to me. My anger continued to build up as I sat there unable to move, speak, or fight and resist these angels' love. The angels didn't intend any harm toward me. Yet I hated them so much! I could feel their love for me in every part of my being. The problem was as I was sitting there looking at their purity and beauty, I was reminded of my own filthiness and that resulted in a torrent of anger and hatred toward them. I didn't want love. I didn't want forgiveness. I didn't want compassion! I wanted destruction. I wanted revenge. I wanted the wrath of Satan himself upon my enemies! I wanted to wield the power of Satan against my enemies and against the angels that were standing in front of me. Alas, I was still unable to move or speak.

The angel who had first spoken to me repeated his promise that it wasn't too late as God would forgive me. My lips were unsealed and with every anger and strength I could muster, I screamed, "NO! I WORSHIP SATAN!!" In the twinkle of an eye, I was transferred to the edge of a high mountain cliff. Everything was covered in a darkness that could somehow be felt. For an instance, I was enshrouded in a blanket of pure darkness. I turned toward my left, and I suddenly saw the two angels in midair. Their enormous and beautiful wings spread to either side of them. Every inch of them emitted a beautiful and pure bright light that was unlike anything I'd ever seen before. Their light illuminated my surroundings, and for the first time I noticed that I was not only on a mountain cliff, but was standing on the very edge of the cliff with my back to what looked like a mighty fall. For all I knew, the abyss could have been 2 or 2000 feet deep. I had no intentions of finding out. Where was this cliff located? Why was I even here? These were the questions that were going through my mind.

The light that the angels were emitting was the only source around me. The light made an entrance to a cave visible, about 60 feet from me.

One of the angels spoke to me and said, "It's still not too late. He will forgive you, just trust in Him and let yourself fall." I couldn't help but be in awe of their beauty and purity. Their faces shining so bright and it seemed as if tears were falling from their eyes! Could it really be that those were real tears being shed for me? The angel's voice was full of emotion and love. However, there was just no way I was going to take a jump into the abyss. I turned and looked toward the cave and stared at it for a few moments. He repeated his words: "It's not too late. He will forgive you, just trust in Him and let yourself fall." I hadn't moved from where I'd been standing at the very edge of the abyss. I was aware that with just a half step backwards, I would fall.

From a Christian perspective, I understand that I was being asked to take a leap of faith into the unknown. I was being challenged to trust God even in circumstances of darkness and uncertainty. However, I had no faith in God. I had no trust in God. I only had faith in what I could see, and what I was seeing at the moment was a dark abyss. I also felt as if it was too late for me. The seeds that Satan had planted years ago had already blossomed and given its fruits. At the same time, I was taken aback by the two angels. How could I ever compare myself to one of them? I was covered in filth and I knew it. I knew I was a sinful man, a man undeserving of even the slightest sympathy, let alone anything good. I would never be pure like one of them. The sins of my past could never be forgotten, let alone forgiven. I felt a pulling at my heart, but it was too late for me. I finally told them with full strength: "NO I WORSHIP SATAN!" The moment I said those words I heard a loud and powerful laugh coming from inside the cave. The laugh was so strong and powerful that I almost fell off the cliff. For the first time throughout this whole encounter, I felt the demonic presence that I had become so accustomed to. I turned toward my left where the angels had been just a moment ago; they were no longer there.

Without the angels' light I was blinded to everything that was around me. I could still hear the laugh coming from inside the cave as I felt the demonic presence beginning to creep all over my body. Had it been there the whole time? Could it have been that the angels' presence had overpowered the evil? Was that the reason I was only now feeling it? I hadn't moved so I was still aware that I stood at the edge of an abyss. Whether I could see it or not, I knew it was there. I turned toward the entrance of the cave, and I saw that something was coming out. From where I stood, it had the shape of a man. The laughter continued to reverberate out of the cave, loud and powerful. He headed straight towards me. He emitted a light that was nowhere as bright or pure compared to that of the angels. I noticed that my current emotions were the exact opposite of what I'd felt in the presence of the angels. The man continued to approach me and stopped about three feet from me. He came close enough for me to clearly see his details. Behind him, I could see the shadows of two acolytes following him. They looked like moving shadows as they emitted no light. The first thing I noticed about the man in front of me was his size. He was much taller than I was and probably stood at about 10-12 feet tall. He held a commanding presence. He had the demonic eyes that were always solid with no pupils. I had never come across a demon of this size and build. He was enormous! His body was covered in scales as if made of black snake skin. He was extremely muscular with the snake skin wrapped tightly around each muscle. His face was hard and was a mixture of snake- and human features. He had no clothes on, yet had no genitalia. He didn't get any closer to me. He just stood there laughing with his strong and powerful voice that shook me to my very core. I don't believe this demon was Satan himself in a different form. Instead, he was probably a high ranking demon in the monarchy of Satan. I dropped to my knees in front of this powerful demon and bowed my head. I could hear the two acolytes that were behind him stirring around, yet never saying a word. When I dropped to my knees, he finally stopped laughing, and for a few moments there was nothing but silence all around me. I don't know which was worse, the silence or the penetrating laughter I'd heard just a second ago. He then said in a voice that was strong and bone penetrating, "STICK OUT YOU HANDS!" His voice was even more horrible sounding than his laugh had been. I extended my arms out to either side as if forming a cross. He grabbed my hands and pressed his huge thumbs in the center of the palms. I felt an incredible burning sensation traveling throughout my entire body. I closed my eyes and screamed in pain as the pain pulsed through every inch of my being. The pain didn't last very long, and when I opened my eyes, I had been transferred to a whole new place. The demon who had been standing in front of me was now on my left. I turned to see behind me and saw the two acolytes about 10 feet away. They were both bent down in a crouching position. I took a breath of the heavy and thick and very HOT air. As I breathed in, it burned my sinus and throat. I could feel it as it traveled through every inch of my system burning everything along the way until it reached my lungs. My lips were dry and extremely chapped because of the aridity and heat of the place. My eyes also felt as if they, too, were on fire with no moisture in them. I'd felt a strong demonic presence where I'd just been; however, what I was feeling in this place was something completely different. What was I even doing in this place? I observed my surroundings, and noticed a red mist that hung in the air like a red fog all around me. Nothing moved, even the fog that was hanging in the air was stationary. I looked up toward the sky and saw nothing – no sun, no clouds, nothing. In the distance, I could see a mountain. The demon stood like a statue, and his eyes were fixed on it. He seemed to have a serious and stern attitude about him. Was the mountain our destination? I didn't know how much longer I could stand being in this place. Every breathe I took seemed to be getting hotter and heavier than the last. I felt as if death was encroaching on me every time I inhaled the air. My goodness! The burning sensation was unbearable.

I tried to focus my vision on the only thing I could somewhat see and that was the mountain in the distance. The demon turned and acknowledged my presence. Until this point, all he'd done was staring at the mountain. Our eyes met and even though he had no pupils, I could sense that we were not just looking at each other. Rather we were looking into each other somehow. I could somehow see and feel the desperation within him, even though he was a demon, perhaps even a high ranking one. Suddenly, he raised his right hand and pointed toward something that was to my right. I focused my vision in the direction and tried to concentrate. My eyes were burning. I closed them for some seconds, but it didn't help at all. I again tried to focus in the direction the demon had pointed. YES! There was something moving far ahead of me. Only it was moving so slow that at first it seemed to just blend into the land. From what I could see, it appeared to be a canal. I followed it as best as I could and it led toward the mountain. I looked at the mountain and back at the canal, and suddenly everything became clear to me: The mountain was a huge volcano! This explained the heat. When I understood these things, I turned toward the demon as I wanted to ask him what this place was, why he had brought me here, and its meaning, but the demon and his acolytes had vanished. I was in this instant alone. I took in another breath and then I finally woke up. My hands felt numb as if I'd slept on them. I moved my hands to flex them and to get the blood flowing again. I saw red marks at the center of my palms – they were at the exact spots where the demon had put his thumbs. The marks raised many questions.

It took me several years before I realized that I was shown the Lake of Fire that God has prepared for Satan, his demons, and for all who choose to reject the sacrifice made for us by our Lord and Savior Jesus Christ (Revelations 19:20, 20:10-15, 21:8). Presumably, the demon standing next to me had such a serious and dire expression on his face as he, too, was feeling everything I'd been feeling in that place of torment. The only difference had been that they knew the place while I'd no idea. I've often wondered if that was their first visit, or if they had been there before and were only being reminded of what their futures held. I had been shown what awaited me if I continued to live in rebellion against Jehovah God.

Years later, as I continue to study the word of God and walk with Christ, I have learned a few other things about the vision. For example, the place had been deserted because the time had not yet come for Satan and those who have rejected God to be thrown into the Lake of Fire to be tormented eternally (Revelations 20:10).

In the following years, I have heard people proclaim that hell is not a real place; however, I can attest to its existence and that the spiritual world and demons are real. I speak out of my own personal experience, and perhaps this is the reason why I was shown the place such that I could relate the information to others; this I've done from my small cell on Texas death row. After the experience, I still remained unchanged as Satan had a stronghold on me. I also felt as if my life was coming to a close. Self-medicating no longer worked. My health had deteriorated in a major way. Besides the weight gain, I had constant migraines and nausea. Every part of my body ached from knees to my back and shoulders. I was still mad at the world and everyone in it, including myself. I no longer had control of my life. I was controlled by anger and depression like a puppet being controlled by a puppet master.

CHAPTER 19:
IT IS TIME TO DIE

In November 2014, I was once again moved back to the A-pod, though this time I was housed in the B-section, which is right next to the men who have execution dates. They are housed in what is called "Death Watch." That year, I had several friends who were on Death Watch with execution dates. During those years it was possible for inmates to run a wire as thin as human hair from one cell to another (no matter how far) and connect that wire from radio to radio and use it as a walkie-talkie. Since we were not allowed to recreate as a group, the wire helped us to stay connected with one another. The guards and rank didn't like that we were able communicate freely and they often destroyed the wire whenever they saw it. They claimed it was a security risk for them, alleging it was used to plot against them, which was untrue. If an inmate wants to hurt a guard they will do so without the need of a wire. It's been done many times before. When I arrived on the A-pod I was allocated cell number 26, which was literally four cells away from Death Watch. My good friend Rolo was only two cells away from me. He was executed on March 7, 2017, but praise be to God that before he was executed he gave his life over to our wonderful Lord and Savior. He was truly snatched from the hands and flames of our enemy, and by God's mercy and grace he is today enjoying peace in the presence of God. We'd get drunk every weekend, and he really opened up to me during that time. It really hurt me deeply when he was executed, but my spirit rejoiced at the thought that he had finished the race and is with our Lord in heaven. I had three other good friends that were on the run with me, and when Rolo got moved to another cell, I hooked up on the wire with them. They had a wire going into Death Watch and were connected to the radio of some of my friends who had execution dates. In total there were seven of us on the "line." Three of them had execution dates while four of us didn't. I can honestly say that all of us were alcoholics, or at the very least had a drinking or addiction problem. We'd spend days and nights drinking and/or popping pills or doing other drugs that were smuggled into death row. Days would turn into weeks and the execution of my friends got closer. We continued to watch as fellow inmates walked out of Death Watch and to their deaths at the Walls Unit. In all my time on death row, I had never drunk as much as I did during those months. It is a hard situation to be with friends who know that they don't have much time to live – and no hope. It is even harder when you know that they are not dying from an illness, but are being put to death on purpose. This was something that was extremely hard for me to deal with, and I wasn't even on death watch. I can only imagine what it was like for the men who had a time and day for their day of death.

As the days went by with alcohol, drugs, and executions, the dates of my friends on the line were getting closer and closer with every day that went by. Time continues to tick away despite the situation around us. The first of my friends to be executed since I moved to the A-pod was MM. He was not on the line with us, nevertheless we had grown close as the years went by. He had been described by the state of Texas as a hit man for a prison family who was cruel and ruthless. If this were true or not I don't know, as I never saw that side of him. I knew him as a man who was willing to help the men around him who were unable or didn't have the means to pull themselves up. When he was executed, it was a hard blow for me to accept. I believe his execution was the first step on my final spiral down rock bottom. My response to his death was the same as my response to everything else in my little world. I drank and took pills until I could no longer feel the pain of losing him, or until I was able to forget it.

The three who had an execution date were scheduled to be executed just weeks apart from each other. When one has an execution date, the person usually follows the media as much as they can, hoping to hear news of some kind of action in the courts or change in the laws that will save them. As it happened, the local media announced that the Texas Department of Criminal Justice was running out of the drug used for executions. It was reported that there wasn't enough of the drug to execute the next several people in line, meaning they had more executions than they had drugs for.

When a person's execution date is approaching, their attorney sometimes begins to throw all kinds of last minute appeals at the courts in an effort to be granted a stay of execution. Some attorneys choose not to submit any and basically abandon their clients at the end. At other times, it is the inmates themselves who don't want any last minute appeals. Why? Some don't want to place their hopes in what they believe to be impossible, while others are ready to move onto the next life.

The news of the drug shortage brought a kind of black cloud over the line when we hooked up to talk. While everyone attempted to keep the atmosphere as light and cheerful as possible, it was not an easy thing to do when death was looming on the horizon. The problem was that if the first person who had an execution date was successful with his last minute appeal, then the state would have enough drugs to kill the next in line. On death row, formidable camaraderie is built behind the walls, like no other place on earth. Perhaps it is because we all find ourselves in the same situation, fighting both the state and an eventual execution, despite our different crimes and sometimes nationalities. The State of Texas wants to kill us all. The first execution date arrived for those who were on the line with me. It was a friend whose nickname was

BB-gun. He suffered from paranoid schizophrenia. He often believed that the guards were plotting against him in some kind of conspiracy. He also believed that they would secretly go into his cell and move his stuff around, or hide stuff inside the cell just so he'd have to look for it. Although he was mentally ill, one thing was for sure: He loved his friends. In the end, he asked his attorneys not to file any last minute appeals. The weekend before his execution date, we threw him a party as best as we could. We made tacos from food bought in the commissary and some desserts. We all had plenty of hooch, pills, and even some weed that had been smuggled in. The day of his execution before they came to get him for his last visit at 8:00 a.m, he smoked his last joint before leaving the cell, and from what I was told he didn't even attempt to hide the smell. After all what more could they do to him? The saddest part of all this is that he had an uncle who had a master's degree in divinity. Yet my friend left this place without accepting our Lord Jesus Christ into his heart; however, I can only wonder where his mind was at while he was at the Walls Unit and when he was placed on the gurney. I can only hope that in those final moments as he lay there with poisoned needles in his arms, he gave his life over to God through faith in Jesus Christ. Perhaps God in His Mercy touched his heart before he took his last breath.

There were six of us remaining on the line. We all felt the pain and hurt of losing one of us, but the days were quickly passing and the next execution date was quickly approaching. There wasn't much time to sit and mourn. So those of us that remained on the line continued to drink, take prescription medicine, or use drugs, attempting to do everything we could think of to cover the hurt and pain we were feeling. None of us would ever mention the pain we felt after seeing another friend walk to his death. Yet, we all knew the pain and hurt were there. It had nothing to do with machismo; instead, it had to do with having to face the reality of where we all were and our own impending future.

The local news continued to report that they didn't have enough execution drugs to carry out all the scheduled executions. Unfortunately, state representatives also continued to comment that they were sure they would find the necessary supply in time. And find they did. Shortly after, another friend on the line was scheduled to be executed. We called him, Silo. He attempted to remain strong willed when we'd hook up, but I began to notice that he would often drift off during conversations. He was still physically there with us, but I believe his mind was into thoughts of his sealed fate. The last weekend before his execution, we threw a party with what was available to us. We had plenty of food to go around plus hooch, pills, and drugs. Regrettably, we had nothing that could bring peace to the man's heart.

After that weekend leading to his execution, he stopped drinking and taking pills, though he continued to smoke weed as he said it helped his nerves. We'd hook up on the line every day, even though he was busy writing farewell letters to his loved ones. The night before his execution date, he told us that he would get on the line with us for the last time at 6:00 a.m., just to say goodbye. He had filed some last minute appeals, but the bloodthirsty courts had already turned him down. So unless some kind of miracle happened, it would be the last time he hooked up with us, at least in this world.

I woke up early on the morning of his execution. I fully intended to talk to him one more time. I felt I owed him that as he had become a good friend. However, when I woke up that morning I couldn't motivate myself to connect to the line. I was tired of having to say goodbye to friends who were being executed. I knew it had never been about "justice" but rather revenge, plain and simple. Revenge was nothing new to me – I'd grown up in Chicago after all. I was beginning to see that this was just evil for evil no matter how people attempted to justify it to themselves. Silo walked out of Death Watch at exactly 8:00 a.m. I heard when he walked out as everyone hollered out his name as he was leaving the pod. I just couldn't bear it any longer. I saw him walk out for the last time. Those of us who were left on the line continued as if nothing had changed. We continued drinking and doing everything possible to mask the pain of yet another friend who had been put to death, all the while knowing that he would not be the last, and that the next one was just around the corner. We kept our feelings tucked away in our hearts. Silo had been raised in a Catholic home, so at the very least he'd heard of who Jesus Christ was as he was growing up. Whether he accepted the sacrifice of the cross made by Jesus Christ at the end, I cannot tell. Only God and Silo know. There was still one more friend on the line who had an execution date, and we called him Hammer. He still had a couple of weeks before his end, and there was at least one more scheduled execution before his. According to the news we'd heard, the "Justice" Department had run out of execution drugs. However, a new supply had mysteriously been found from a supplier who requested anonymity. According to what we'd heard in the news, they had found a compounding pharmacy that was willing to supply them with the drugs they needed to carry out executions. So the killing machine was reloaded once again to continue without any interruptions. The state had several more executions scheduled for that year and all of them were going to be carried out.

For the first time ever, thoughts of suicide began to slowly creep into my mind. Never before had I thought of hurting myself, others yes – all the time – but never myself. The cutting I had been doing was only because I needed blood to do my rituals. I wasn't cutting myself because I wanted to feel pain or because I had a need to "feel something," as I've heard some describe to me why they have done it. I just found myself so tired of life. I was tired of the cell, tired of feeling alone, tired of the everyday routine that came with being locked up. I was tired of seeing my friends walk out of this place never to come back. More than anything else, I was just tired of living. I never imagined that those words would ever enter my mind, and yet they got me when I least expected it. While there are many who cannot relate to suicide, I am also sure there are many who can. To those who can, I have this to say: It is a merciless lie from the pit of hell to believe that life is no longer worth living, or that you are useless, or that the world would be better off without you.

Satan had put all these feelings in my mind, and I believed them all – that I was nothing but a burned burden to my family and to society. What good could I ever do from behind the prison walls? There were many nights during which I would drink tremendous amounts of hooch and take so many pills that I was sure I would not see the next morning. I was certain that my body would just shut down in my sleep, and I wouldn't have to face another day. Then morning would come. I'd wake up full of hatred and anger because there was a next morning. I can't pinpoint the exact day in which I began having suicidal ideations. From when I became aware of it, I began to contemplate how I was going to take my own life.

My friend Hammer's execution date arrived. He was the last one of my friends with a date. As the state continued to kill my friends, they also continued to fill up the cells on Death Watch as they were being emptied. It was an unending cycle that continues to this very day.

As had become customary, on the weekend before Hammer's scheduled execution, we threw him a party. On that dreadful day, I didn't hook up with him. I'd made up my mind to no longer say goodbye to my friends. It was not that I no longer cared, but rather I could no longer take it. I was told that before they came to get him for his last visits that morning, Hammer slammed back some bottles of hooch. Hooch and pills were the way we dealt with problems and tensions of being on death row. I don't believe it is much different from many people who are on the other side of these walls. They, too, deal with the stresses of this life with alcohol, street drugs, or prescription pills. We run to the things that Satan puts before us that look desirable, or we are able to cover our pains even if it's just for a moment. Satan will put anything in our lives in order to lead us away from the one and only who is able to do all things, including giving us peace, joy, and victory over whatever it is we may be going through, and that is Jesus Christ.

I've come to realize that material goods can only cover up our problems and the tensions for a short while. Sooner or later all the repressed memories and anger will resurface in one way or another when one least expects it. There is only one who exists who can release us from all our tensions, heal our wounds, and give us true freedom from depression, oppression, addiction, alcoholism, and every other chain of bondage that the world and Satan have placed upon us. It is only with the power of the Holy Spirit and through the name of Jesus Christ that we can be truly free, and live a life of abundance in peace and joy.

My friend Hammer was taken to the Walls Unit in Huntsville. The Walls Unit is where more than 500 executions have been carried out since the 1980s. I can only imagine the demonic presence both in the execution room and in the city surrounding the prison. Executions usually begin at 6:00 p.m., unless there is some kind of appeal pending in one of the courts. As he was awaiting a ruling from the courts, he sat in a tiny cell several feet away from what is called, The Death Chamber. I can only imagine what was going through his mind as he sat there waiting to take those few steps to his death. A few minutes before 5:00 p.m., he received a phone call from his attorney, telling him that he'd received a stay of execution! He was brought back to death row and returned to the same cell on Death Watch. We were all excited to see him again, even if it was in a prison cell on Texas death row. It was not often for someone who went to the Walls Unit to return. The next day, we hooked back up on the line, and he told us everything that goes on from the minute you leave Death Watch and get to the Walls Unit. After he had told us about his experience, I unhooked my wire and that was the last time I ever hooked up with anyone on Death Watch. I had many other things on my mind. I felt a profound loneliness deeply within me, and I kept telling myself that it would all come to an end soon.

On one lonely night as I was drinking and listening to the radio, I scanned through a magazine as I usually did at night. I got bored with the magazine and put it away. Immediately after, more or less on an impulse and without much thought, I began to make a rope out of nylon while I was consuming large quantities of hooch. When I had made about five feet, I tied a noose on one end and tied the other end to the cell-light grill and placed the noose around my neck. It was finally time to die and blow out my candle. Without giving it a second thought as if in a trance, I let myself fall into a sitting position, but as I dropped the rope broke – either I was too fat or because the grill was too sharp, thus cutting the rope. I hadn't planned to hang myself that night. I don't even know where the idea had come from. I got up and, without even thinking about it, I began to make a thicker rope. Before I could finish it, I passed out.

By this time, I'd been cutting myself for a long time and was used to it. Nevertheless, I didn't want to cut my veins because I wasn't sure how fast I would bleed to death. I didn't want a guard to pass by the cell and see me in that position and rush me to the unit's infirmary. I knew if I ended up there, I'd be put on suicide watch, and from there I wouldn't be able to do anything. Instead, I asked a friend of mine who had a drug mule for some help. He'd been the one smuggling many of the drugs to death row. He assured me that whatever was put in his mule's hands, I would receive. With that in mind, I asked someone close to me in the free world to find me some heroin. Growing up in Chicago, I'd experimented with different drugs, but I'd never tried heroin. I'd only heard of how easy it was for a person to overdose on it. I was certain if I could get enough of it, I could easily overdose and bring my life to an end. I was also quite certain it would be a quick and painless way to go. Knowing what I had in mind, my contact on the outside refused to help me. However, this was prison and there were many different ways to obtain any kind of drug one might be looking for. I'd determined in my heart that this was my best route and option – so I ordered some heroin. What I had not counted on was that God already had His own plans for my life. He'd allowed me to see the Lake of Fire. He'd allowed me to enter and see demonic realms, and He'd even allowed me to see and make pacts with Satan, but at the end of it all His purpose was, and is, going to be fulfilled. Praise God!

CHAPTER 20:
"I WAS THERE"

My package never arrived! It was always either somehow captured out in population before being brought into my building or the mule was unable to bring it into the unit. Other drugs like weed and meth were coming in regularly. It was only my package that was somehow being detained. In the end, the mule got caught and he was fired – that was the end of that option.

Despite this, it wasn't the end of my suicidal thoughts. In my own mind I felt as if death would bring me freedom from all my problems and pains. I believed I'd find peace in death – after all I still served Satan. I was sure I would not be tortured in hell as I had a signed pact. As I sit here and write these words down, a verse that describes how I felt at the time comes to mind: "We have made a covenant with death, and with Sheol we have an agreement, when the overwhelming whip passes through it will not come to us, for we have made lies our refuge, and in falsehood we have taken shelter" (Isaiah 28:11). I didn't exactly believe that I was hiding behind treachery or falsehoods; instead, I had a pact with Satan, and I was safe from the overwhelming scourge, torment, and torture. Today my belief is that the plans of Satan are always death for those who serve him. It truly makes no difference if you are a practicing Satanist or if you practice occultism of some kind or not. If a person finds themselves living outside the perfect will of God and doesn't have Jesus Christ as their personal Lord and Savior, then it's the same as being a Satanist or practicing the occult because you will end up in the same exact place where they will end up – hell. Satan's plans are always oppression and death for all. How many times have we not heard of the rich and famous committing suicide? The reason being they were living outside the will of God. I have learned that, sooner or later, everyone who lives like that will consider or attempt suicide at one point or another. Why? Because those are the only plans Satan has for all. Satan knows that once a person is dead there is no more hope for them, no more asking for forgiveness, and there is no more repenting of one's sins. There is nothing outside the presence of God. Satan himself and all his fallen angels will be tormented in the Lake of Fire. It is only Jesus Christ that came and dwelt among us, suffered, died, and rose again so that we may have life in abundance.

We must make our decision while we are alive in this world – a conscious decision of who it is that we will serve. Our options are very easy: we will either serve God, Satan, or ourselves. Yet there is only one that will lead us into eternity in the presence of God.

As for me, I continued to contemplate on an easy way to take my own life because although I wanted to end it all, I didn't want to suffer. The weeks and months continued to pass me by and I found myself in desperation and anguish. There was no one I could go to for help. There was no one I could go to for advice. I felt alone like never before. My family continued to visit me, but even their company was of no help to me. Even in their presence I felt completely abandoned and alone. I couldn't even sleep at night without taking pills or drinking myself to sleep. I wasted entire days just thinking about suicide and death. I'd become obsessed with death. I didn't realize that had God allowed me to go through with suicide, my next step into eternity would have been severely worse than anything I was going through in this life and at that moment.

Death row continued to do what it was designed to do which is kill, and I continued in my downward spiral falling deeper and deeper into depression with each execution. I continued to watch as they moved more and more friends of mine to Death

Watch with execution dates.

Despite all that was taking place, my life would soon take a turn that I could never have envisioned. I had and have a family that was calling on the name of the Lord and interceding for me, night and day. There were many members of the Body of Christ whom I'd never even met who were down on their knees in fasting and prayer for me. All of them united in one spirit calling out the name of the Lord and interceding for me, despite me having performed every kind of ritual and blasphemed God in every way possible. I believe that because of the prayers of my family and the saints, God had mercy on me.

While there may be many who desire my death in the name of "justice," it is Jesus Christ who has given me life in abundance. Sunday, July 13, 2015 was exactly eight years from the day I'd been arrested. My life had changed dramatically from that day forward, eight long years ago. On this day of my "arrest anniversary," my life would once again change forever.

On Sundays, we were never allowed to go to the exercise yard. I enjoyed Sundays as it was usually nice and quiet. The guards were not trying to do any more work than they were required to do – so we were left alone most of the time. On that Sunday evening, I was standing at the cell door talking to a friend who was just a few cells away. Neither of us was really talking about anything. We were just living in the past for a little, talking about memories of our lives outside the walls. As we were talking, he mentioned that his medication had been upped. He was on some kind of downer medication, and he told me he'd taken two pills and had been on cruise control for the last three days. I asked him to send me a few so that we could be on the same ride. He told me he would send me three, but to only take one so I could see what kind of reaction they had on me. I kind of laughed to myself at that and told him to stop trying to be my nurse and send me what he had. He sent the pills and when I got them, I didn't even look to see what they were – I just washed them down with a cup of coffee.

I'd been taking prescription drugs for many years and had probably tried all the ones that were available to us. I'd never been a big fan of "downers" in the free world, but behind the walls they were usually the easiest pills to come across. I guess TDCJ doesn't want inmates to be all hyperactive. Eventually, I went to lie down to kick back and listen to the radio. I looked at the clock and it was about 7:00 pm. I'd taken the pills an hour before. About two hours later, my stomach began to feel a little queasy. I'd felt that way previously when I'd taken other pills, like Zoloft, so it wasn't really a big deal to me. I continued to waste time and listen to music for several more hours. My stomach didn't get any better as time passed. As I lay there, bored and listening to the radio, out of nowhere I suddenly felt as if someone punched me in the brain. It felt as if a wave and fist of pain hit my whole body. It began at the very top of my head and moved downward throughout my entire body, until the very tips of my toes. I grabbed my head with my hands, swung my legs to the side of the bunk, and sat there for a few seconds holding my head. When the pain began to subside, I got off the bunk and began to pace the cell, intending to just walk off whatever it was I'd just felt. The alarm clock showed that it was exactly 11:00 p.m. It had been around five hours since I'd taken the pills. I thought that perhaps they'd had a delayed reaction, or that I might be experiencing a bad trip. Perhaps I should have listened to my friend and just taken one. All I could do now was to ride it all out. I started pacing the cell from the bunk to the cell door, which is not much pacing at all. It's about three steps from the bunk to the cell door, and that is taking small steps. As I was pacing the cell I began to break out in a cold sweat, and my mind began to run. I wasn't feeling nauseous or sick or anything like that. Even my stomach was fine. I didn't even have a head ache. The wave of pain I'd felt come over me had just pulsed through me and quickly went away. I couldn't explain what had happened. Being that it was July, the cells were usually pretty hot as the temperature outside usually remains in the 90° to 100° – and that makes the temperature in the cells even hotter. However, the heat wasn't the problem. Instead, I was having a hard time understanding what I was seeing running through my mind. I could see flashes of my past and certain memories zoom through my mind from times that seemed like a lifetime ago. I continued to pace the cell and tried to focus on the memories and thoughts that were coming and going. It was quite disorientating as I couldn't focus on a single thought. The flashes were moving so quickly that I could only pick up one here and there, before it moved on to the next one. I couldn't control my own thoughts. The more glimpses I caught, the further they went back into my childhood. It was almost as if my life was being displayed in rewind on an old VCR tape. My memories kept going further and further back, and as I attempted to stay focused on a certain memory – it was quickly replaced by another. At some point, my memories all came to a sudden stop. My thoughts stopped swirling through my head, and all was still for a few seconds.

I was covered in sweat, yet I continued to pace the small cell back and forth. My mind seemed as if it was a big TV screen that had displayed my life in rewind mode, and then, without any warning, things changed instantly: They began to move forward starting with a memory I'd never in my whole life ever thought about. I saw myself at my old grammar school in Chicago, named Plamondon. I was in preschool and I was probably about 4-5 years old. It was sometime during the Christmas Season because I could see Christmas decorations hanging in the classroom. The classroom door opened, and walking in came Santa Claus out of all people. I saw the kids ran up to him with big smiles on their faces. Every kid seemed so excited. However, as I looked closer at Santa Clause I saw that it wasn't really Santa! (just kidding – he wasn't a demon in disguise). In fact, it was my friend's mom who had been dressed up as him that year. I continued to pace the cell while the memories moved forward one by one, without missing a mark.

The next memory was of my older brother and me sitting on the top stairs of a house where we lived on Chicago's Southside. I was about 5 or 6 years old, which means my brother was 10 or 11 years old. We were both sitting on the top of the stairs playing with something, when out of an alley came two gang members. The one on my left slowly picked up his right arm and pointed a gun at us, which was concealed inside a brown paper bag. The man standing next to him said, "Hurry up and just do it!" As a kid, I was oblivious of all that was going on around me. I just continued to sit there and play with whatever toy it was I was playing with. Later, I did ask my brother about this event, and he described it to me exactly as how I'd seen it almost three decades later. When my brother saw the gun, he jumped up and grabbed me by the hair and flung me inside the house through the front door, before diving through the door himself. I saw myself begin to cry as I didn't know why my brother had just pulled me by the hair. As I was seeing this, I then saw the gang members run back down the alley they had come from, and then I heard a voice inside my head, saying "I was there." My life began to unfold itself like this, day after day and moment after moment. I saw myself in the very first fight I'd ever been in. It was with a kid named Pedro who was in my kindergarten class.

As my memories flashed before me, it seemed as if I'd been fighting throughout my whole early childhood. I saw when I began to carry all kinds of weapons to school, some were homemade others were not. I saw how gangs would chase me after school – even though I wasn't in one at that time.

I saw myself using different exits in the school to leave, trying to stay one step ahead of them. I believe that I was never caught by them, not because I was faster or smarter than they were, but for the reason that there was someone who already had His own plans for my life and was protecting me even then. My memories inched forward and I saw when I walked into an alley surrounded by gang members. When we walked out of the alley, a car was slowly passing by and did a drive by on us – at that moment I heard the same voice, "I was there."

I continued to pace the cell dripping sweat all over the floor. I tried to tell myself that it was just the drugs I'd taken and to just kick back and enjoy the ride. It was impossible – I didn't enjoy one single moment of the madness. I'd never taken anything like these before – that is – if it were the drugs that had induced my mental state of madness. For a moment, the thought crossed my mind that perhaps I was dying. I'd heard it said before that when a person is dying their life flashes before their eyes. "Could this be what was happening to me, was my body slowly shutting down?" I asked myself. The thought that this could possibly be true just brought a smile to my face.

I also saw myself at the age of 12 or 13. A rival gang tried to murder my friends and me while we were in front of a local pizzeria in our neighborhood. They jumped out of their car and started running towards us while shooting. I managed to jump into the back seat of the car we had arrived in. I landed on top of four girls who were with us that night. As I lay on top of the girls, the back window suddenly exploded as a gang member was shooting up the car. I then saw him run up to the passenger's side of the car. I was seeing everything in slow motion, and I didn't miss a single thing. I saw him slowly raise his right arm and point the gun at the passenger's window in the back and then shoot. The window exploded as the bullet made its way through it and struck me on my right side in-between two of my lower ribs. With the window broken, I saw him take a couple of steps forward. He thrust his gun through the window and placed it two or three inches away from my head and pulled the trigger, but the gun didn't fire! He pulled his hand out, and they all began to run back to their car. As the shooting had stopped, yet not knowing if they were just reloading, I saw one of my friends run toward the nearest street. The girl who was in the driver's seat was finally able to peel off. As I saw the shooting unfolding in my head, I heard a voice, saying "I was there." Every moment of my life was passing through my head as if it was a movie on the big screen. I clearly saw every time that death was near me and attempting to touch me by either gang violence or accidents. I could see how most of the accidents that had occurred had been caused by demons attempting to end my life. Yet no matter how close death got to me, it was never allowed to touch me because God had stayed the hands of death. It wasn't only the times that death had been near me that flashed through my mind. I also saw all the violence that I had caused growing up in the streets of Chicago. I saw all the hurt and all the pain and suffering I'd caused. What was it all for? For a street that never belonged to me? For the right to live in a neighborhood? I saw that it had been for nothing. It was all just a waste of time and a waste of a childhood. Tears began to fall from my eyes.

While the minutes and hours had been advancing throughout the night, so were my memories and life. I don't think it is possible for me to sit here and write down every act of rebellion I relived. It was close to three decades of sins and wrong decisions that I had made and saw that night. Today, I acknowledge these sins and feel sorry for them. All were committed in ignorance and rebellion against my Lord and Savior Jesus Christ, and as King David once said, I also say, "Do not remember the sins of my youth, nor my transgressions; According to Your mercy remember me, For Your goodness sake, O Lord" (Psalms 25:7, NKJV).

Step by step and year by year were passing through my head. Eventually, I saw myself arriving at the county jail, and from that I saw myself bending the knee to Satan in worship and supplication. I observed everything. I saw as I fell deeper and deeper into alcoholism, and finally I saw myself so far gone and so lost to the world that I was holding a noose in my hands. I then felt and heard the same voice I'd been hearing all night long: "All your life Satan has been attempting to take your life, but I have been there. I've covered and protected you. Yet you have chosen to serve Satan. You have chosen to bend your knee to Satan." Hearing those words tore my heart into pieces. I knew it was the truth. Time and time again, God had extended His loving hands towards me, and over and over again I'd chosen to reject His love and mercy. Uncontrollable tears were falling from my eyes. I didn't know exactly what was happening to me, but things seemed to have gotten out of control. I wanted the night to end and the sun to shine – but mostly for the rapid succession of memories to stop. Tears continued to fall from my eyes as if they were fountains spewing water. I was completely covered in sweat and tears. My body felt weak, and my knees felt as if they would give up on me at any moment, yet I continued to pace. I felt that if I stopped, I'd never be able to walk again. I went into a state of denial, trying to reject the memories. However, I couldn't deceive myself – those had been my own memories, and it had been me in every one of them. My memories brought me all the way to the very night before when I'd gotten the pills. I saw when I'd taken them, and all the way to the exact moment

when I was about to take the next step in my small Texas
death row cell.

CHAPTER 21:
LORD PLEASE FORGIVE ME!

Three decades of my life had passed through my mind in a single night. I continued to ask myself how it was possible. I was on the verge of collapsing. The alarm clock showed 5:30 a.m. I'd spent the whole night pacing the cell in a cold sweat. I finally did collapse on the bunk as my legs could no longer hold my weight. A few minutes later, a guard came to the cell and asked me if I'd be going to the shower. The prisoners in my section didn't have recreation time on Mondays, so we could only leave the cell for a shower. I really needed one. My mind was still running, though I was beginning to calm down. At around 7:45 am, a couple of guards came to the cell door to escort me to the shower. When they had escorted me back to my cell, they slammed the cell door shut. For the first time, I heard when the door's lock pin fell into place. Suddenly and for the first time I knew that the cell door was locked in place. I knew I was trapped and it frightened me. I felt like a caged animal. Anxiety and paranoia fell on me like never before. I put my hands out through the open slot, and the handcuffs were removed from my wrist. The guard closed the slot and went on his way, while I just stood there for a few seconds. I looked around the cell as if I was seeing it for the very first time. I was seeing everything with so much clarity and detail as if the specks that were obscuring my vision had been removed. I thought maybe it was just my eyes that were playing tricks on me from a lack of sleep. I noticed some writing on the wall. I'd been in the cell for close to six months and had never seen it before. Unbelievable. When I saw the writing, I don't know how I knew, but somehow I knew, or at least felt, that those words had been written by someone who was dead. I felt an overwhelming physical pain come over me, as I stood there and thought about the person who had written the words. For some reason, I could feel his pain, loneliness, and the load that he'd carried. I couldn't figure out why I was feeling this way or why I even cared.

The sun was shining bright. There was no reason why I should still be feeling the effects of the drugs. I figured all I needed was some sleep. However, I knew I wouldn't be falling asleep anytime soon, despite the fact that I was physically drained and exhausted. It was a little after 8:00 a.m. and the guards were about to do the "8:30 a.m. count." As I rested on the bunk, I was still having a hard time accepting what I'd seen and everything that my own mind had revealed about me. Why had Satan taken such an interest in me? Was it like this for everyone? Was he after everyone's life with such determination? His interest in me was perplexing to say the least. I attempted to convince myself that this whole thing had just been a side effect of the drugs. Suddenly, my eyes closed and I heard someone say, "You need to change the way you live." I opened my eyes instantly! It'd sounded as if it had been said by someone inside the cell. I got off the bunk and went to the door, thinking that perhaps I'd overheard something a guard had said as they had passed my cell. I didn't believe I'd heard correctly. It couldn't have been what I thought I'd heard. There was no one on the run, and the exercise yard was empty. Everything was actually pretty quiet as most of the people in the section were still asleep, since we didn't have any recreation that day. I went over to the sink and splashed some water on my face. I thought I might have just imagined it or something, so I went back down again on the bunk. I kept thinking why had the memories resurfaced all of a sudden? Was it possible it was caused by some chemical in the pills? I had no answers to these questions. As I contemplated the situation, I heard the same voice again: "You need to change the way you live!" The voice was strong and I felt it reverberate through my body. It carried such a

185

power behind it like nothing I'd ever experienced before. Not only did it carry a profound power behind it, but also an incomparable authority. However one thing was certain: I was absolutely sure of what I'd heard.

I called out to my neighbor and asked him if he'd said something or had heard something. He replied, "Like what?" I told him, "Never mind." The last thing I wanted was for him to think that I was losing my mind although that was exactly what I thought was happening. I just didn't know if I was in the process of losing it, or if I had already lost it and that I was hearing voices. I splashed some cold water on my face and took a look at myself in the mirror. I looked normal. I mean I wasn't seeing anything unnatural, I was just hearing voices! I splashed some more cold water on my face, took a deep breath, and tried to make sense of what was happening. No matter what may be going on in a person's life behind these cell walls, and no matter how a person may be feeling back here, there is only so much we can do for ourselves. The staff, medical personnel included, only cares about one thing – that you are breathing. Everything else is secondary, especially if it's going to cost the state money, after all this is a for-profit-system.

I still had hope that I could somehow force myself to fall asleep, and maybe, just maybe, I would wake up and things would all be back to normal. I'd seen many in this place go nuts, and I didn't want to end up that way. The reality was that it seemed as if I was on the fast track to insanity. Perhaps I'd taken too many pills and had pushed my mind over the limits. I was desperate for this to come to an end, whatever "this" was. My mind zoomed in on the words I'd just heard. God, was I really going crazy? Had these walls finally gotten to me? Was I really losing my mind? Or even worse: Had I already gone down the rabbit hole? As I pondered these questions, I heard the same voice again repeating the same message. For some reason, I began to repeat those words over and over: "I need to change the way I live. I need to change the way I live. I need to change the way I live ...." Indeed, I needed to change the way I was living. The third time I heard the voice and the message I didn't even bother to get off the bunk as it was no longer necessary. I knew exactly whose words they were.

I believe my heart had known who was speaking to me from the very beginning. I was in denial. I couldn't fight it anymore. I accepted that it was the Holy Spirit who had spoken those powerful words to me and had been talking to me all night long. What I'd gone through that night had nothing to do with the pills I'd taken. Something much stronger than any drug had been working in me. The Holy Spirit had been preparing me for a choice I would soon have to make.

I felt the weight of all my years of rebellion and rejection. My heart felt heavy as if it was being weighed down with an anchor. It felt as if each of my evil deeds and ways had its own weight that had been placed on my chest and was pushing down on me. I couldn't help but gasp for air as I felt suffocated. I couldn't take it anymore. I couldn't deal with the pressure. All the self-medicating, the drinking, the depression, the oppression, I didn't want any of it anymore. I wanted help. I needed help! With tears streaming down my eyes and with all the strength I could muster, I cried out to God with my entire heart, saying, "LORD PLEASE FORGIVE ME! CLEANSE ME OF MY SINS. I CAN'T DO IT ON MY OWN ANY LONGER, PLEASE MAKE ME NEW. I NO LONGER WANT TO LIVE THIS WAY. I KNOW I DON'T DESERVE YOUR FORGIVENESS OR YOUR LOVE, BUT HERE I AM LORD. I GIVE MY LIFE TO YOU. DO AS YOU WILL WITH ME LORD, BUT PLEASE HELP ME!"

CHAPTER 22:
DEPART FROM ME SATAN; I AM A CHILD OF GOD

Growing up in a Christian home, I've known the word of God since my early childhood. My parents would take my siblings and me to church eight times a week. My father, being a musician for most of his life, taught me how to play the drums at about the age of seven. As a kid, I didn't mind the worship part of the service as I was playing the drums along with my father on the guitar while my brother played the bass. As an adult now, I thank God that I had parents who were believers. They knew the importance of taking us to church from an early age, even if we didn't always want to. They knew that one day we would be adults and make decisions on our own, based on the foundation of God's teachings imprinted in our hearts. As a child, I knew all the old Bible stories – from David and Goliath to Daniel and the Apostle Paul. I thought they were all very exciting. As an adult, I had grasped the meaning behind the stories. However, I just didn't want to either believe or accept them. I wanted to live my life as I wished. I didn't want some God up there in heaven telling me what I could and could not do. Regardless of my aversion and denials, the Holy Spirit transformed me that night. As I have grown in my faith and belief, the Holy Spirit continues to work with me. I can often clearly feel when He is directing me in a certain direction or towards a certain decision. Frequently, I can hear Him inside of me when He wants to relay a word to me. I have fallen in love with His presence. It is a feeling that I never want to come to an end. One day, I will be surrounded by this feeling for all eternity.

As I lay there covered in tears, I had given my all to the Lord. I cannot say that I instantly felt relief wash over me – neither will I say I suddenly knew that everything was going to be okay. I didn't feel forgiveness wash over me, or the Holy

Spirit come upon me like a dove. I felt none of that. Instead, I felt heart broken. I thought about what I'd put my family through, and the thought of that made me shed more tears. I felt miserable, ashamed, and an embarrassment, not only to my family – but to myself.

I had seen the horrible person who I'd been my whole life. Yet I wondered if I could really change. Was there any hope for a poor soul like me?

As all this was going through my mind, an old Bible story popped up in my mind. The Holy Spirit had put the story of King Saul on my mind. It says, "For rebellion is as the sin of witchcraft, and stubbornness is as iniquity and idolatry. Because you have rejected the word of the Lord, He also had rejected you from being king" (1 Samuel 15:23, NKJV). The last statement is the one that really stuck out to me. I had truly rejected the word of the Lord – basically my whole life, and though my cry to God had been truly sincere, I believed that the Holy Spirit was telling me that this was my final opportunity. On the other hand, I didn't feel as if the Holy Spirit was in anyway forcing me to accept Christ as my personal Lord and Savior. The decision was mine to make. The Holy Spirit had just made my options really easy, and the decision was no longer a tough one to make. I knew that I really needed to change the way I was living. It wasn't just because the Holy Spirit had told me so, but he had brought me into the realization that I was living a life that wasn't pleasing in the eyes of God and the people around me. I had been blinded all these years.

I didn't feel like I could move off the bunk. My legs felt completely numb from my hips to my toes from all the pacing I'd done for countless hours. I kept thinking about the story of King Saul and how the Spirit of God had departed from him. I didn't want that to happen to me. I'd given it my all when I'd made a decision to practice Satanism and nothing good had come out of that. I wanted to give God my all, and with this thought running through my head, I finally fell asleep. I woke up late `1at around 7 p.m. I got off the bunk ready and wanting to make changes, but I didn't know where to begin. Growing up in a Christian home, I knew that Christians prayed and read the Bible. Those would be my first steps. I was now *in* Christ Jesus as it says in 2 Corinthians 5:17: "Therefore, if anyone is in Christ, he is a new creation; old things have passed away; behold all things have become new, (NKJV)." After getting the cell in order, I got on my knees with a new purpose, and I bowed my head in prayer to the one true God. I didn't really know how to pray or what to say. So I began by just saying thanks to the Lord for another day, for my family, for His love, and for the opportunity He had given me.

After praying, I got a hold of my Bible. It was old and tattered from all the years of packing it up to move from cell to cell. When I'd gotten it out, it had many pages that were folded in and stuck together. The cover was discolored and peeling away. The only reason that it had survived as long as it had was the fact that it had been a gift from my parents, and I'd never had the heart to throw it away.

It had been more years than I could remember since the last time I had read the Bible. I began to read the book of Matthew in the New Testament. I figured I'd read the New Testament straight through, one chapter per day. As I was sitting on the bunk preparing to read, I looked up and towards the cell door. There I saw two satanic medallions I had hanging from a hook next to the door. I kept them there so I could quickly put them on every time I left the cell. I got up and, without a second thought, threw them in a trash bag by the door. I knew what my next step would be. I went inside the locker under the bunk where all my property was stored, and I took out every book I owned, including the occult books. I had accumulated quite an extensive library over the years. I began to tear up the books one by one, page by page. I didn't want to leave them whole for someone else to pick up and read. They had done enough damage already that I wouldn't wish on anyone. I then took out all the other materials I had used to carry out my rituals. Among the items I had were an altar cloth, parchment paper, a ritual feather for writing, and several others. One by one I tore, broke, and took apart each and every one of them. After finishing with all of my occult materials, I moved on to all my fiction books. I knew that the books had nothing to do with the occult. Nevertheless, I was tired of filling my mind with murder, fornication, thievery, violence, and everything else that goes into fiction books. If it didn't have anything to do with God, I didn't want it in the cell with me. The only book I kept, after all was said and done, was my Bible.

When my trash bag was overflowing, I began to throw stuff right out of the cell and on to the run. My neighbors must have thought that I'd gone crazy. At that moment, I didn't really care what anyone was thinking of me. If I was going to serve Christ then I was going to do it in the right way.

From that day forward I set apart a certain time, every day, to spend with the Lord in prayer and to study His word. It was a discipline I knew I had to teach myself through practice and consistency. For the first time in years, I was actually feeling happy. I thought it might be because I had actually taken the first step in embracing change.

After cleaning the cell out of the things I felt no longer belonged in my life, I went in the locker to get myself something to eat as I had missed both my lunch and dinner trays. I looked through it and noticed that I still had some cans of orange juice. Orange juice was what I'd been using for years to make hooch. I just pushed them to the side and didn't think anything of it. It was already late in the day so after making myself something to eat, I just went back to sleep. My legs were still sore from the pacing I'd done the whole night. I woke up the next morning, which was a Tuesday, and did as I had determined to do. As soon as I was done with my normal morning routine, I got down on my knees and prayed to God, thanking Him for another day and for my family. I then started reading the Bible. I was determined to keep this up and make it a routine from now on.

I opted for an early shower rather than exercise that day. When I came back to my cell, I wanted to make myself some breakfast. When I opened the locker, I noticed the cans of orange juice. Perhaps it was just the routine I'd taught myself for so many years, so when I saw the cans I decided to cook them for the following weekend. I attempted to justify it by telling myself that these would be my last bottles.

Jesus Christ tells us, "If your right eye causes you to sin, pluck it out and cast it from you; for it is more profitable for you that one of your members perish, than for your whole body to be cast into hell. And if your right hand causes you to sin, cut it off and cast it from you; for it is more profitable for you that one of your members perish, than for your whole body to be cast into hell" (Matthew 5:29:30 NKJV). Should we really believe that Christ wants us to go around blind and maimed? Absolutely not! What Jesus is telling us is that we must deal with sin in a drastic and quick way. Sin is not something that we can slowly wing ourselves off. If this were the case, I could have never slowly stopped drinking or taking prescription drugs. An addict can never slowly wing themselves off drugs. We must learn to eliminate many things if we are to follow Christ. The Word also tells us in Genesis 39:12 that Joseph literally ran from temptation. Although it landed him in prison, he was not willing to sin against God. The Apostle Paul tells us in 1 Corinthians 10:14, "Therefore, my beloved, flee from idolatry."

What exactly is idolatry? It is not just the bending of the knee to some idol made of wood, gold, or any other material. It is anything that impedes us in our walk with Christ. It is anything that we love more than we love the Lord, or that we depend on more than we depend on the Lord for. My mistake was in not throwing away the juice the night before. I should have thrown it away and not have left myself an option of having it in the locker. How many times have we decided to serve the Lord, yet we leave ourselves open with options should we want to go back to our old ways. The temptation was too much for me, and I took the juice out of the locker and began to prepare them. I added the extra sugar and all the other ingredients needed to make it into hooch. While I was putting everything together, I felt sick to my stomach. I felt that what I was doing was wrong. I felt guilty. I pushed those feelings aside and continued to do what I wanted to do. According to my own plans, I would have the hooch ready for the following Sunday. Since it was hot in the cells, it would not take the whole week to ferment.

I continued to stay true to my prayer and study time. I didn't really know how to pray, and would sometimes feel a little strange or silly during prayers. I also didn't really understand everything I was reading. Being determined, I continued reading no matter how I felt. I knew there were obstacles on my journey with Christ. However, I also knew that I'd just begun my walk, and it would take some time for our relationship to grow and develop. To make the relationship stronger, I stopped listening to music that wasn't Christian. My life was changing. At the same time, I knew that some of those changes that were needed were up to me to make for myself.

The smell of the fermenting hooch really irked me. Sunday came and I was ready to drink. I'd gone the whole week without taking hooch or popping any pills. Physically, spiritually, and mentally I was feeling great. I took the hooch out of its hiding place and placed the bottles on top of the table. Because of the ingredients and the way we make hooch, it is necessary to strain it before drinking it. There is a fungus that grows at the bottom of the bottles which helps in the fermentation process. I cleaned out all six bottles. I felt horrible, yet I had butterflies in my stomach as if this was the first time I'd be drinking. After straining them, I placed three bottles back in the locker, just in case I got hit with a random shakedown while I was drinking. My tolerance was so high that I needed to chug two before I could feel anything. I took a short sniff from one of them and it smelled like rubbing alcohol. It made me nauseous. Deep down my heart, I had no desire to drink these bottles, but routines are sometimes hard to break. Before I chugged my first bottle, I remember saying, "Lord if this is really wrong, then let this be juice instead of hooch." I said these words with a sarcastic smirk on my face. Today, I believe that it was the Holy Spirit who had murmured those words out of my mouth.

I brought the first bottle to my lips and began to slam it down. By the second swallow, I could taste that something was off. It didn't have the usual burn. It really tasted like juice! Orange juice! I took another swig and my God – it was straight juice! I took a swig from the other two bottles I had sitting on the table, and they, too, were nothing but juice! I went in the locker and took out the other three bottles and took a swig from each them, and they were all coming up as 100% orange juice. This was impossible! Just a few minutes ago it had smelled like rubbing alcohol. Unbelievably, it didn't even have the smell of alcohol much less the taste of alcohol. If there was a skill I had mastered behind these walls it was how to make hooch.

I took another swig from each bottle, and a big smile spread throughout my face. My last words before drinking these bottles had come true. Though this is impossible before human's eyes, nothing is impossible for our God. I was beaming and had a smile from ear to ear. I realized that again our Lord and Savior Jesus Christ had demonstrated His powerful hands in my life. I flushed the juice down the toilet as I should have done a week ago. Alcohol had done nothing for me since my childhood but brought me pain and misery. I'd used alcohol for many years to numb and conceal the pains and trials of everyday life. This was it – no more!

In all the years I'd spent drinking both in and out the prison walls, the thought that I had a drinking problem and was an alcoholic had never crossed my mind. In the same way, it had never occurred to me that I was addicted to pills. I was starting to see things differently. The Holy Spirit was revealing things to me that I had been blinded to.

In addition to eliminating alcohol and satanic influences, it was also essential for me to make other changes. For example, certain friends I would need to distance myself from, especially friendships that had been founded on drug and alcohol use. On the other hand, I also had friends who had opened up their hearts to me. Friends I'd been able to count on when things got tough behind the prison walls. They were always ready to get tough either with other inmates or with guards and come to my rescue. These were men I knew I could count- and depend on no matter what occurred back here.

I had truly been freed from the shackles of addiction. I had been sleeping without the need of any kind of alcohol or pills in over a week. I didn't want anything to do with any of that stuff any longer. How could I later testify of what God had done to me if I was still up to the same old things? Was I not a new creation? Had I not been born again as the Bible was telling me? I stopped going to the recreational area all together for a while. I'd only go out of the cell to go to the shower. I dedicated more and more time to reading the Bible and really trying to understand it. There were entire days I would spend sitting on the bunk with my Bible in front of my eyes. I continued to pray in the mornings and at night. However, I still felt as if something wasn't right. I felt as if there was still something that was impeding my walk with Christ. I began searching for what it was. I knew it was still early in my walk, yet I could already feel a difference and I wanted more so I was eager to continue. One of the main things, I knew I needed to change was the way I spoke. Every other word that came out of my mouth was a curse- or a perverted word. It was typical prison talk. Even though I was no longer going to the exercise yard, there were still friends who would come and talk with me. When we spoke and I said a curse word, I would feel a stabbing pain in my heart. I'd feel as if someone had literally stabbed me in the heart and a cloud of regret would weigh heavily on me. The Holy Spirit was indeed changing me from the inside out, and I loved it. I went on this way for a while: secluded from everyone and everything that was going on outside the cell I was in. All I did was read the Bible and pray with the occasional song of praise to our Lord.

I still didn't understand everything I was reading. However, I knew that sooner or later the Lord would reveal His word to me, as He did to His disciples in Luke 24:45: "And He (Jesus) opened their understanding, that they (the disciples) might comprehend the scriptures" (NKJV).

I was feeling something that I'd never felt before: I was feeling peace and unexplainable joy. I'd wake up in the mornings no longer feeling hurt and depressed about having to face another day. Instead, I would wake up with a big smile spread across my face. On many occasions, before I even got off the bunk, I already had a sound of praise on my lips to our Lord. No matter how many pills or drugs I'd had in the cell in the past or how much hooch I'd made, I never woke up feeling happy and eager to seize the day. All I wanted now was water from the fountain of living water and the bread of life. I was now sleeping like a conquering king. I was sleeping more peacefully than I'd ever slept before. I hadn't woken up feeling any kind of demonic presence and the thought of suicide was something of the past.

For several months, I remained secluded from the world outside the cell. I'd go to the shower and return to the cell and then go right back to reading the Bible. Little by little, I was beginning to understand more of what I was reading, and every time I understood something new, my heart would be filled with joy. I was also listening to sermons on the radio by preachers who were giving me insights to scriptures.

I was eventually moved again – this time to cell number 25 in the C-pod. By now, the Lord had totally removed my alcoholism, addictions, depression, oppression, and had even purified my language. The anger and resentment toward my family, myself, and the world were gone. God was truly making me over in all aspects of my life. I had approached my walk with Christ and my spiritual growth in the same way that a person might approach exercise and physical health. I wanted to feed myself everything that was Christ filled. I wanted my mind to be renewed. I wanted the light of Christ to shine on me. The same way that exercise gets easier to do as the muscles grow, so did it become easier for me to stay on my knees in prayer longer, and spend even more time reading and studying His word.

However with all that has been said and done, the more time I spent on my spiritual journey, the more I continued to feel that there was something that still didn't belong in my life. I got on my knees one day in the middle of the day and began to pray and ask God to reveal to me what it was that was still holding me down in my growth with Him. While on my knees, the Holy Spirit revealed to me a picture that was under the bunk in the locker. I instantly knew what it was that was still in my way. I say these next words with much shame and embarrassment. Inside the locker, I had somewhere well over 1000 pictures of pornography and a stack of catalogs I'd not gotten rid of. I'd known all along they'd been there – it wasn't something I'd simply forgotten about. Rather it'd been something that I'd not wanted to let go of, but I realized I couldn't serve both God and myself. I couldn't pick and choose the areas I would serve Him in, yet leave a part of my life off limits to Him, There is no such thing as half-stepping when it comes to serving God. I knew the choice I'd made and the difference I'd already felt. I didn't want that to stop and I wanted more.

After I was done praying, I went into the locker and took all the pictures and catalogs out and set them on the table. I flipped everything over so I couldn't even get one final look at them, and I began to tear them up one by one into tiny pieces. When I was done with the pictures, I moved on to the catalogs. I didn't even want the option of being able to reorder them. It had never crossed my mind that along with my alcoholism and addiction to pills and drugs, I'd also been addicted to pornography. God wanted all of me, and that was exactly what I wanted to give Him. I felt I was completely free from everything that had bound me in sin to this world. I finally felt as if I had a direct line to God with nothing impeding my way. Now that my life had been changed, I felt the desire to share what the Lord had done for me with everyone around me. I believe that the desire of wanting to share the gospel of Jesus Christ is a sign of being a servant of Christ. I believe that every servant of Christ, whether they've been serving for 50 years or 50 days, will have the desire to share what the Lord has done for them and continues to do. I was no different in this.

Since arriving on death row I'd largely kept to myself. I've always been a somewhat asocial, even on the outside. I had a reputation of being a serious person, and I was also known as a Satanist who took the practice with extreme seriousness. I was also known to always have hooch and pills and be a pornography seller. What a reputation I had built up for myself! However, it was time for me to start spreading the wonders of the Lord with other inmates.

CHAPTER 23:
I WILL PREACH YOUR WONDERFUL DEEDS OH LORD

I decided it was time for me to begin going to the recreational area again. I wanted to let my light shine as it is said in Matthew 5:16, "Let your light shine before men, that they may see your good works and glorify your Father in heaven," (NCV). How could I share what the Lord had done for me if I never came out of the cell? I began going there again, but this time with my Bible in my hand. The same people who had known me just a few months ago – those who had seen me at my worst – were now seeing a new creation, a new me. My talk was no longer what it used to be. I no longer cursed or used perverted expressions. Everything I said, everything I spoke about was somehow Christ centered. I'd share my testimony of my encounter with the Holy Spirit with anyone who was willing to give me ten minutes of their time. I've had friends tell me that they didn't believe the change in me was real. Some have told me they would sit back and just observe, waiting for me to fall back into my old ways. They are and will forever be waiting because I'm not going back.

I did find it funny when a good friend of mine, who I hadn't seen in a few years, caught up with me and asked what had happened to me. He told me he'd heard a rumor that I had overdosed on some pills and had had a near death experience. The rumor then indicated that I had lost my mind. I can understand why people thought this way. It's a common thing for these walls to eventually get to some people, but, no, I had not lost my mind I had clearly had a spiritual and religious awakening and epiphany. The Bible in 1 Corinthians 1:18 says, "For the message of the cross is foolishness to those who are perishing, but to us who are being saved it is the power of God." I can also understand why it seemed like foolishness to those who were around me: I'd gone from being a practicing Satanist addicted to pills and alcohol to a child of God. I was now a Christian! It didn't really matter to me what people were saying about me, whether behind my back or to my face. All that matters to me is what my Father in heaven thinks of me, and I know He loves me unconditionally. Before giving my life to Christ, I guarded my reputation at all costs. I'd grown up on the streets of Chicago where a reputation can at times keep you alive.

Those who were around me didn't understand the change that had taken place in my life. They didn't understand that Jesus Christ had saved me. They didn't understand that Christ had set me free from my addictions. When they would see me drunk or high, they considered it to be my normal behavior, and I guess that, in a place like this and perhaps even in many places outside these walls, it is a normal way of life. As I was no longer drinking or getting high, I seemed like the one who had lost his mind. In the last few years, I've been called everything from crazy to a fanatic. However, if those same people could have lived the life I've lived, or, better yet, seen the things I've seen, I believe their thoughts toward me would have been different.

I will admit, though, that I am a fanatic for Christ. I say those words with much pride. After many years, I know exactly what Jesus Christ did for me on the cross of Calvary. While I was covered in sin and filth, He chose to bring me out of the pit of desperation and from the muddy murky waters. He then put my feet upon the rock and straightened my steps. How could I not be a fanatic towards a God who did such a thing for me? How could I not serve Jesus Christ with all my heart when He did such a powerful thing for me?

The Apostle Paul speaks to us about spiritual armor in Ephesians 6:11-17. For us who believe that armor is free, it is because the price has already been paid for it. It is only up to us to reach out our hands, take it, and put it on. However, if we are untrained in how to use that armor then it is of no use. The training consists of prayer, fasting, and studying the word of God. We must do our part in training with this spiritual armor, so that when the times of temptation arrives, and it will absolutely come, then we can be prepared and know how to both defend and attack in the spiritual war. Ephesians 6:12 says, "For our battle is not against flesh and blood, but against the rulers, against the authorities, against the world powers of this darkness, against forces of evil in the heavens." Though our struggle is spiritual, it affects us in every possible way in the physical realm.

I used to believe that if we kept ourselves in constant prayer and fasting, Satan's fiery arrows could never make it through our spiritual armor, but this is not always the case. There are times when, no matter how much fasting and praying a person may be doing, his arrows make it through. When that happens it can, and usually does, cause a great deal of pain. Yet, we must remember that we need those arrows to penetrate us every now and then. I know that might sound crazy to some, but it is true nonetheless. If it wasn't for those arrows that bring us trials and tribulations, we would forget that it is because of God that we even exist; we would become dependent upon ourselves and forget about the one who created all things. Whether we have a lot or a little, I believe it is sometimes necessary to be reminded that it is God who gives us the power to create our wealth, as it says in Deuteronomy 8:18, "And you shall remember the Lord your God, for it is He who gives you the power to get wealth, that He may establish His covenant which He swore to your fathers, as it is this day," (NKJV).

I know trusting in the Lord wholeheartedly is not always an easy thing to do. It is not always easy to understand what it is that the Lord has planned for our lives, and it is even harder, at times, to accept what the Lord has planned out for us. However, I can say that it does get easier as we continue to walk with the Lord and grow in His Word. There were many times when I would ask God why He had allowed me to go through the things I've been through. Why did He allow me to practice Satanism? Why did He allow me to fall deeply into addiction and depression to the point of trying to take my own life? Could He not have reached me when I was still free and didn't have a death sentence over my head? The answer is, YES! Of course He could have, and many times He did reach out to me with His loving arms, but it was me who thought I was getting by on my own wit. While in the free world, the thought never crossed my mind that I needed God's help. After all it was my life. There was nothing, I couldn't fix with enough money or knowledge of the situation. What did I need God for? So when God called out to me, I refused to acknowledge His voice and I didn't want to accept what He had to say. Coming to prison became the appropriate place for God to put "Raul Spooky Cortez" to death so that I could be born again as "Raul Cortez servant of Jesus Christ and child of God." Although I have never experienced death as the separation of the soul and body, I have learned to put the flesh to death, and I have also learned that it is not an easy thing to do. Jesus Christ tells us in Luke 9:23, "If anyone desires to come after Me, let him deny himself, and take up his cross daily and follow me," (NKJV). That cross, which Christ speaks of, was made for one thing and one thing only: execution. In other words, Christ is telling us we must put our flesh to death daily by denying ourselves the things that are worldly, and we must be prepared to stand tall every day and deny these things because our battle is new every morning. The Apostle Paul in 1 Corinthians 6:9-10 names the unrighteous, idolaters, thieves, drunkards, extortionists, and others who will not inherit the Kingdom of God (NKJV). That is just to name a few. If we really look closely at even this short list, it is clear that none of those behaviors will bring us peace and joy. Christ tells us to follow Him, and let Him provide us with the things we need, both spiritually and physically. He is the only one who can satisfy all our needs. As for me, now that I've moved on from materialism and have experienced what life is without depression, addiction, and everything else that was holding me bound, I never want to go back to that life for anything in the world. "No one who puts his hand to the plow and looks back is fit for the Kingdom of God" (Luke 9:62). How many times have we not been freed from bondage only to go back and place the same chains of bondage around our own necks? How many times have we not made the decision to stop drinking, smoking, doing drugs, or whatever other vice, only to fall back a few days later? We must understand that it takes a power much greater than our own to remove chains we cannot see with the physical eyes. I don't want anyone who is reading this today to think that once we give our lives over to Christ, our cravings will immediately stop. We must still do our part to resist temptation. Satan is not going to stop dangling worldly pleasures in front of our eyes just because we have given our lives to Him. These temptations are an everyday part of this fallen world, but this is where the Holy Spirit steps in. We must learn through reading the word of God and learning the promises that have been written, so that we can be victorious in the physical world. Prophet Nehemiah says, "The joy of the Lord is your strength" (Nehemiah 8:10). As I sit here after giving my life to Christ, nothing has changed around me. There is still hooch, pills, and drugs everywhere. There is still pornography available to me. However, I took the responsibility of changing my own life. I didn't have the option of changing my surroundings; instead, I do have the option of what I will spend my days doing and what I will feed my spirit. Every one of us must make a similar choice. When I was free, I'd been to church many of times and had been liberated from the chains of bondage. However, I just didn't know how to stay free – as soon as I left the service I'd go right back to the life I'd been living with no effort on my part to stay free or change. As soon as I would step out of the church, Satan would demand my blessing and I would freely give it to him. I had no idea how to fight what I could not see. Like most people who go to a Bible teaching church, I'd heard of spiritual warfare and spiritual armor, but I neither believed in its power nor did I have any idea of how to use it. I'd hear the preachers preach on the power and authority given to us in the name of Jesus Christ, but I didn't believe that either. I thought it was just something they said to get the congregation roused up, which it usually did. This was something I would have to learn on my own through the Holy Spirit and apply it to my own life. What is the use if we learn something, yet never apply it when it counts? Or if we have something in our possession, yet never reach for it when we need it the most? It wasn't until I began to apply what I was reading in the Bible that I began to see results. If we are to walk by faith and not by sight as the Word tells us to do in 2 Corinthians 5:7, then it is us who need to move our legs and take those steps forward. My biggest problem in the free world was not that I didn't know about Christ and His Word – I just didn't believe in His power or in the power that He has given us. I didn't believe that the spiritual realm could influence our physical dimension. Having seen and interacted with the heavenly realms and the demonic world, how can I not believe? I have dealt with many tough situations as I'm sure everyone else has. I have faced many powerful demons, some willingly some not so willingly, and even had legions of demons dwell in me. One thing, I have learned, is that no matter the size and power of the demon that we are facing, no matter how terrifying and challenging the trial that we find ourselves in, we must learn to always keep our focus on Jesus Christ. It may not be an easy road, but it will eventually lead us to eternal life. Apostle Peter says, "Lord to whom shall we go to? You have the words of eternal life" (John 6:68). While many walked away from Christ, Peter knew He was the only way. Who else can we go to? After we've tried everything the world has to offer us, who can we go to? Where can we run to? In my case, nothing I tried ever did me any good. Christ is truly the only one that can help us get through any situation we may be facing. No matter what it may be, even if it's a matter of life and death, He is the one who is sitting on the throne and always will be. After so many years lost to drugs, alcohol, depression, perversion, and sin, and wasting so many years looking for what was missing, I can honestly say that I've found it all in Jesus Christ. Nothing in this world was ever able to give me what Christ has been able to give me in abundance, despite my surroundings. As I sit in this prison cell with a death sentence over my head, I enjoy a peace that the free world was never able to give me. I'm freer today in this death row cell, surrounded by concrete walls and electrical fences, than all the years I spent in the "free" world. As of this writing, I've been physically locked up for over a decade, but I imprisoned myself since the age of 11 by walls I began to build around myself through alcohol, drugs, and various other materialistic desires. Believe it or not, there are many today who find themselves in a worse prison than I find myself in today. They find themselves in a prison with Satan as puppet master, pulling on the strings he has placed in their lives. Anything and everything that empowers the body over the spirit can become a personal prison, whether it is drugs, alcohol, sex, pride, work, money, or even food. Satan will use these things to attempt to direct and manipulate our lives to distance us from God's ways. We must remember that none of these things will ever bring us any lasting peace or joy, and no matter how much a person may deny that peace and joy are what they seek in life, they are just lying to themselves. What good is money and power if one cannot sleep at night? What good is it to have numerous, expensive possessions, yet not have love in one's heart and life? There is only one way to receive everlasting peace and joy in abundance. That way is Jesus Christ: "For Jesus is the way the truth and the life" (John 14:6). Christ wants to change our lives for the better. I don't understand why I couldn't see that for so many years. All we have to do is accept what He has to offer us. It is us that must accept the sacrifice that He made for us on the cross of Calvary. The word tells us that all have sinned and fallen short of the glory of God (Romans 3:23). So how do we come to repent? How do we accept the gift from God? It's easy. Romans 10:8-10 says, "The message is near you, in your mouth and in your heart. This is the message of faith that we proclaim. If you confess with your mouth that Jesus is Lord, and believe in your heart that God raised Him from the dead, you will be saved. With the heart one believes, resulting in righteousness, and with the mouth one confesses, resulting in salvation" (HCSB). Christ has already done the work for us. He came down to us and took our sins upon Himself in a physical way. He took all of our rebellions upon His own body. By His precious blood, we have been redeemed. It wasn't because we deserved it, or because He owed us a debt of some kind. In fact, the Word tells us in Romans 5:8, "But God demonstrated His own love toward us, in that while we were still sinners, Christ died for us" (NKJV). It also says in John 3:16, "For God so loved the world that He gave His only begotten Son, that whoever believes in Him should not perish but have everlasting life" (NKJV).

God loves us with an immeasurable love and continues to love us the same way today. It doesn't matter what you've done in your past. The magnitude of our past sins doesn't matter. It doesn't matter what kind of lives we used to live. God loves us in that state and has called us to Him through Jesus Christ. Christ, Himself, said He did not come for the righteous – he came for the sinner (Matthew 9:13). This is truly a reassuring verse for us. There is nothing that we may have done in our past that He doesn't know about, and that He is not willing to forgive us for. As I continue to grow in my walk with Christ, I've learned that everything we freely give to our Lord, He accepts with one hand and gives it back to us in abundance with His other hand. For example, the Lord asks for our lives, and He gives us eternal life (John 3:16). He wants our love, yet He has given us His only begotten Son (John 3:16). He asks that we humble ourselves before Him, yet He says He will exalt us before man (Matthew 23:12). When it comes to material things, He asks for a tithe of what we earn – yet He says that He will open the windows of heaven for us (Malachi 3:10). The list goes on and on. It all comes down to putting our trust in Christ in every aspect of our lives. After all, He is the author of life. I can wholeheartedly say that there is nothing like serving our Lord. There is nothing like being free in Jesus Christ.

I've had it said to me that the Bible is just a book of do's and don'ts. I disagree. As believers, we voluntarily leave certain lifestyles behind us because we love Christ and because we choose to place Christ in the center of our existence. When we spend time in prayer, we do it because we want to talk with God who is our Father. When we sing to our Lord, we do it because we want to worship and praise our God for what He has done for us. Even when we go to church, we go because we want to be united with the body of Christ and share in the bread of life, which is Jesus Christ. All these things are done voluntarily and out of love for our God.

Serving Christ behind these walls is not an easy task. There are many who take humility and meekness as a sign of weakness. I have been mocked for going into the recreational yard and singing praises to our Lord. There are some who keep an eye on me in an attempt to point a finger at "the Christian." They still don't understand that I changed my life because I love the Lord. Even though, I may look like a fool in their eyes when I'm out there singing and praising the Lord, it is Christ who I am pleasing and not the men around me. When we accept Christ into our hearts and it is sincere, changes are inevitable. I cried out to God several times, but it wasn't until I was honest with myself and sincere that I really began to see changes. When repentance is sincere, and we begin to really seek the face of God, change inevitably happens and we begin to see the world and its fallen state differently. The bar scene no longer looks attractive to us, we'd rather spend time in church seeking the face of God. We no longer feel comfortable around our old drinking buddies because we are no longer on the same boat in life. We might begin to feel more comfortable around brothers in Christ who are strong in the Word. Things like spending time watching TV no longer appeal to us as we'd rather spend time reading and studying the Bible. It is not because the Bible tells us we need to do these things, but because we see and feel the changes in ourselves and those changes bring happiness.

I understand that the readers of this book might be thinking this is a little too extreme. That's understandable. However, if we really think about it and ask ourselves: "Why do I need change?" We'll see that if we really felt that all was good, we wouldn't be looking for change to begin with. Specifically, we seek change since we recognize that something is missing in our lives, whether it is peace, joy, freedom from some kind of addiction, or something else we may be going through. We recognize that something is not right or that something is missing that we have not been able to fill. We also come to the point where we appreciate that everything we have tried has not worked, and that we must try something different – Jesus Christ.

We must understand that the battle is much greater than ourselves, so we need a power much greater. My questions are these: "How much of our lives are we willing to let Satan steal from us before we accept that something is wrong? How far must we fall? What point must we reach?" In my own case, it was necessary to come to Texas death row and attempt suicide. It is only because of God's love and mercy that I am here today and able to share my testimony with you. It is only because of the power of God who suspended the hand of death.

Every day, we hear story after story of where the hand of death has not been suspended. I truly believed that in death, I would have found tranquility and other things I desired, but it had all been a lie that Satan had placed in my head. If my problems and struggles were many here, how much would they have been multiplied after death and outside the presence of God?

CHAPTER 24:
THE DEVIL NEVER SLEEPS

Suicide has unfortunately become an ugly part of today's culture. Today, there are many parts in the civilized world that offer "state assisted suicide." In a world where courts have deemed it a right to be allowed to kill a baby still in the womb, killing them outside the womb when they are of age is no longer a big deal. We have become desensitized to death, suicide, and murder as the world has continued to grow cold. The Word of God gives us four examples of suicide, three of which were committed after a betrayal. The first one is found in 1 Samuel 31:4-5 in which it is described that King Saul took his own life during a war with the Philistines. What we know about King Saul is that the Spirit of God had departed from him some time before (1 Samuel 16:14). We also know that God refused to speak to him anymore (1 Samuel 28:6). King Saul was tormented by an evil spirit (1 Samuel 16:14-23), and we know that prior to going out to battle the Philistines, he consulted with the medium of Endor (1 Samuel 28:6-11). In those days not only by the law of God but by King Saul's own decree, it was a capital offence to consult with a medium (1 Samuel 28:9). So is it not reasonable to believe that a demon drove King Saul to commit suicide? After all, the Spirit of God was no longer with him – rather an evil spirit had possessed him. As I've said before, the plans of Satan are always death at any cost. The second example I found is in 2 Samuel 17:23, where we can read that the prophet, Ahithophel, betrayed King David then went and hanged himself. The third example is found in 1 Kings 16:15-19. Here, King Zimri conspired against King Elah and then struck him down. When Zimri saw that the troops had made Omri the King over Israel and that the city was captured, he ran into the palace and burned it down on himself. The fourth example is probably the most known and is found in Matthew 27:3-5. Here, Judas Iscariot betrayed our Lord and Savior for 30 pieces of silver. After attempting to return the silver, he also went and hanged himself. I don't believe it is a coincidence that three out of the four examples given to us were committed after they had betrayed someone. Satan will make us betray ourselves or others if we allow him to. He will dangle thoughts of death in our minds, making it seem that death is the answer to our problems, or in some cases the only answer.

Satan wants us to believe that life is not worth living. He wants us to believe we are worthless and useless. He wants us to believe that we are nothing but a burden to our families and to everyone around us, and that the world would be better off without us. Satan tortured and occupied my mind with all of these lies until I finally believed each and every one of them. We must remember that Jesus Christ gave up His own life and shed His own precious blood for us. This wasn't done so we could live a life of agony and despair. It was done so we could live a life of hope, peace, and joy. This is His promise to us (John 14:27; 17:24). Jesus Christ spoke of Satan's intentions in John 10:10 where He said, "A thief (Satan) comes only to steal, (he wants to steal our peace, our joy, our blessings, and even our lives if we allow him to) and to kill. I (Jesus) have come that they (us) may have life and have it in abundance" (HCSB). Suicide is never the answer! The answer is Jesus Christ. The three things, Jesus mentioned in this verse, kill, steal, and destroy, all point in one direction, and that direction is completely opposite of what God wants for us. It really is possible to live a life full of peace and joy no matter what storm in life we may find ourselves in. The decision is ours to make. Do we want to live for Christ and trust in Him? Or do we want to continue living and trusting in ourselves? Never in my testimony have I said that serving Christ is an easy thing to do. I still find myself in a death row cell with many temptations. Whether you are a believer or not, the fact is that our greatest enemy is Satan.

Through the power of the Holy Spirit, I can see Satan's attacks, and I know how to defend myself. We must always remember that we live in a fallen world and whether you believe it or not, we are surrounded by demons and fallen angels at all times. Some of these fallen angels are very powerful and defend their territory at all costs. The more I have studied the Word of God, the more I have learned that we, too, have been given powers. Those powers are much stronger than the powers of any demon. The Word tells us in Colossians 1:16, "For by Him all things were created that are in heaven and on the earth, visible and invisible, whether thrones or dominions or principalities or powers. All things were created through Him and for Him" (NKJV).

There are many who believe in God, yet don't believe God. To believe in God is to believe that there is a God out there who created the heavens and the earth, but to believe God is to believe His word. To believe His word is to believe in all the promises that have been written to us and for us. This is why it is important for us to know the scriptures from our early childhood.

We are taught to depend upon ourselves for everything. We are taught that a good education will get us a good career. A good career will get us a good salary, and with it we can buy almost all the things this world dangles in front of our eyes. For the most part it is true. What we are not taught is that all these things will only bring us material wealth, but not what we desire the most, which is everlasting peace and joy. What is almost never mentioned is that the Word tells us that God gives us the power to gain wealth (Deuteronomy 8:18). Without misunderstanding what I am saying, there is nothing wrong with having wealth and a good career so long as we don't place them before God. There are just some who have forgotten that in the beginning God created the heavens and the earth! This generation has been taught world history, but our educators have left out the part where the Israelites were in the desert for 40 years depending solely on God who provided for their every need (Deuteronomy 8:2-4). We have forgotten that in the name of Jehovah, the Israelites conquered giants, took over kingdoms, parted the sea, knocked down walls, and destroyed entire armies without weapons. It is even written about Elijah who called fire down from heaven and stopped the rain from falling, and all this was done in the name of Jehovah! Furthermore, more than anything else, many have forgotten that God is the same yesterday, today, and will be the same tomorrow and forever. It is us who have forgotten who Jehovah really is. We have something that they didn't have in the Old Testament days. We have the Holy Spirit that dwells inside of us. When we really come to believe that the father, son, and Holy Spirit are the one and the same, then we come to believe that we have the power of Him who spoke the heavens and the earth into existence because He dwells inside of us. We must believe these words not because you are reading them now, but because they have been written in the scriptures. Jesus Christ told us in Mark 9:23, "If, you can believe, everything is possible to the one who believes."

Satan knows exactly what he is doing. He's been up to the same tactics for millenniums. He has perfected his trade and always knows when we are at our weakest moments. It is an everyday struggle that we must learn to deal with. However, it gets easier as we grow in our walk with Christ. No matter what it is that Satan tempts us with, it will never last as his solutions are a quick fix. The problems will remain within your psyche.

Satan will always supply us with a quick fix to all of our

problems, and try to make us believe it is the answer we had been looking for. He does everything in his power to hide the fact that Jesus Christ is the answer. In my own life, it wasn't a very elaborate scheme. My journey began by just wanting to find truth, somehow that lead me down the road to Satanism and attempted suicide. Satan also filled my head with much doubt; for example, he made me doubt God's power, my own abilities, and even my own worth. He wants us to doubt that we could ever be forgiven for our past sins. The Lord rebukes that lying serpent! The Word tells us in Hebrew 10:16-17, "This is the covenant that I will make with them after those days, says the Lord, I will put My laws into their hearts, and in their minds I will write them and their sins and their lawless deeds I will remember no more." There is only one way, and that way is Jesus Christ – for He is the Way, the Truth, and the Life, and nobody comes to the Father except through Him (John 14:6).

CONCLUSION

I've been imprisoned for well over a decade. I gave my life to Christ on July 14, 2015, and my life has never been the same since. There have been many trials and tribulations that have appeared, but my whole outlook on life has been changed forever. As of July 2020, I still find myself on Texas death row with a sword at my neck. To some, the thought of having a death sentence over their heads is horrifying. Perhaps I should be more concerned about my current situation, but I thank God that I am not. I thank God that He has filled me with so much peace and joy that my surroundings are no longer an issue to me. As crazy as it may sound, I thank God that He has allowed me to come to this place. I came to the house of death and I died in this place, and I was then reborn a child of God (1 John 3:1). The Apostle Paul tells us in Romans 8:28 that all things work together for the good of those who love God and have been called according to His purpose. I truly believe this from my small cell in the middle of nowhere. I've had the privilege to share my testimony with people from across the world. There have been many times, Satan has attempted to make me stumble and fall, but I often remind myself that it is I who asked God for a testimony. About two weeks before I was arrested, I was in my apartment in Orlando, Florida, high and trying to fall asleep. I was staring at the ceiling, and I called out to the God that I didn't want to serve, and said, "Lord I don't have a testimony like many of Your servants have, but if You gave me a testimony I would testify about it."

Well the Lord has definitely given me a testimony, though this is not what I had in mind! However, it is with much joy in my heart that I share my testimony with the world. It is with much joy that I share all the things God has done for me. It is with much joy that I share the places and experiences that Christ has rescued me from. People can call me crazy, they can call me a fanatic, or even a hallelujah – it doesn't matter to me because I am all those things and much more.

That God could and would use a death sentence for something good proves He is faithful to His word. Truly if God is for us, who can be against us? (Romans 8:31). My life and this testimony are proof that we truly are more than VICTORIOUS in Christ Jesus (Romans 8:37). In the same way that God did it for me, He wants to do it for you and everyone in the world. It doesn't matter what you've done in the past. The past is in the past – let's leave it there. We must not wait until we are sitting in a prison cell doing a life sentence or sitting on death row. We must not wait until we are hospitalized, or until Satan has stolen our family and even our desire to live. Today is the day of salvation (2 Corinthians 6:2). Today is the day that the Lord has given us. Tomorrow is not promised or owed to any of us. Whether you believe or not, heaven and hell are real places, and we are all destined for one of them for all eternity. Which one will you choose for yourself? You can have peace and joy today, and all it takes is coming to the feet of Jesus Christ and accepting the sacrifice that He made for us on the Cross at Calvary. I don't bring this testimony to a full end because Christ is still working in my life, and my testimony is far from over. As long as I have breath in my lungs, and my heart is still beating, I will continue to serve the Lord Almighty and proclaim the greatness of our Lord and Savior Jesus Christ. As my parting words, I say that Jesus loves you, as do I.

PEACE OF CHRIST

Acts 20:24,
But I count my life of no value to myself,
so that I may finish my course and the ministry
I received from the Lord Jesus,
to testify to the gospel of God's grace.
Amen.

PICTURE GALLERY

Raul playing the drums while his dad is singing and playing the guitar.

Raul flying his boss's plane.

Before his arrest, Raul traveled frequently with his company.

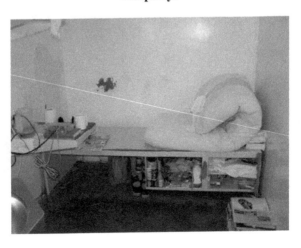

A typical cell on Texas death row.

A toilet-sink combo which all cells on Texas death row are equipped with.

Another view from inside a cell.

A tray slot through which food is delivered into each cell.

Cells as seen from the outside.

Many cells have burns marks like these. Inmates set their
cells on fire to get the attention of an officer

A view of a cell door closing.

An outside 'rec' yard.

A view of the visitation room.

A recent picture of Raul on Texas death row.